No Barrier

How the Internet Destroyed the World Economy

Bob Brill

Table of Contents

Dedication

This book is dedicated to my father Jim whose work ethic surpassed any I've ever known.

To those who believe in Freedom and that Freedom comes at a price, be it economic, political or the rights of man.

Introduction

"The Internet is like a fast moving brush fire burning across the earth, fanned by the winds of greed. No one wants to extinguish it and you can't control it, but a way must be found to contain it. Keeping in mind the parameters of free speech and all the good the Internet does, Free Speech must be protected from those who would use and abuse the Internet for personal gain at the expense of others around the world."

Bob Brill

Forward

The Internet is the new frontier. We have lived, and prospered, because of it. But, in many areas – politics, privacy, copyright, and trade – the impact is just being understood.

The U.S. Supreme Court grappled with how free speech in the Constitution can be balanced with the interests of artists protecting their copyrights; the fight between Google and Wikipedia, on one side, and the movie and music industry, on the other, showed how complicated it would be to pass antipiracy legislation. The Arab Spring showed the power of social network sites in passing instant communication to protestors. And, GPS tracking through the Internet has been instrumental in powerful military equipment, including predator drones and in locating missing persons, not to mention finding our way home.

"No Barrier " is a tour-de-force about the Internet's impact on the loss of jobs. No one who wants to promote jobs or growth in the international economy overall can responsibly say that the Internet has not benefitted the world. It has. The only problem is that the United Nations and individual countries have to deal with the massive dislocation of jobs as a result of the development of the Internet. With all advancements in society and inventions there is a downside and retraining and education are essential. The upside with the Internet is incredible. It has allowed poor families to communicate with their relatives in different countries, without running up a phone bill; families have been reunited over long distances -- a father and daughter perhaps -- when someone gets ill. In the political spectrum, the Internet revolution has revolutionized revolution. This book explores the next steps -- and the big picture questions that must be raised.

Pamela Falk, Ph.D., J.D.

CBS News TV & Radio

Hunter College in the City University of New York

About the Author

Bob Brill is an award winning journalist with over 40 years in broadcast and print. He's a news anchor at a major Los Angeles radio station, working in this large market for more than 20 years. As a National Correspondent and later L-A bureau chief for the UPI Radio Network, Bob covered major events all over the U.S. through Asia. Well known for his versatility he's reported from sporting events including World Series, Super Bowls, the Seoul Olympics in Seoul and play-by-play. He also worked for the L-A Times. Among his honors is a distinguished Edward R. Murrow Award.

As an entertainment reporter Bob covered nine Academy Awards presentations and dozens of Emmy's and Grammy's. On the business desk Bob reported on occasion for the UPI Radio Network and published his own widely respected newsletter. The Brill Report focused on the business aspects of sports memorabilia and related fields. He became known as the industry watchdog and broke numerous stories, some of which were picked up by large, main stream newspapers.

Bob started several businesses and was in on the early days of the Internet. He has watched many of his friends either thrive on the Web or lose their businesses because of it. An accomplished traveler he's been to 27 countries and has passed on the love of traveling to his three children. He's also written several screenplays. His first book (Schiffer Publishing) hit retail store shelves in 2009. "Fan Letters to a Stripper: A Patti Waggin Tale," details the life of the former burlesque queen and her major league baseball playing husband, Don Rudolph. His third book "Al Kabul; Home Grown Terrorist" is a novel set in the future. Bob lives in Los Angeles.

The Destruction of Business 101

"I can destroy any industry, anytime, any place and I don't have to be wealthy to do it!"

Why? Because I can.

How? Via the Internet.

Reason? There is no barrier to entry to doing business on the Internet!

Bold statements to be sure but totally accurate in today's world of E-Commerce. When Al Gore invented the Information Super Highway back in the early 1990's he envisioned the Internet as a place in space on earth where information and commerce would flow freely at instantaneous speeds globally. It was going to create a new paradigm and re-create the way we do business. It has.

Thank you Mr. Gore.

No, really, thank you Mr. Gore.

Unfortunately not even the former vice-president of the United States and Academy Award winner could have foreseen what has happened. There are many folks to blame for the current state of the world economy. Some will blame the housing market and speculators, some will blame terrorists and their impact on the global economy, some will blame the Chinese and still others will blame plain old greed. This is after they blame each other's political party. Some will put the banks at the heart of it and they are correct to a point if you wish to skip ahead to Chapter 15. Feel free to do so.

Before we proceed hacking up the Internet and the World Wide Web let me first point out, as many of you may be no doubt seizing this moment, the Internet has created an incredible amount of opportunity for entrepreneurship. It has created many millionaires and even billionaires before and after what became known as the first "dot-com bust." There are those who will read through the pages of this book and take bold shots and cite case after case where the Web brought millions of people into ecommerce who never sold a widget in their life. It did and has and will create opportunities much like those in the real non-virtual world. There is no denying this. However, this book will explore what that same Internet did to destroy businesses, jobs and lives and to eliminate jobs which will never come back. It wasn't only in the name of progress but rather in the name of greed in some cases and stupidity in others.

The truth of the matter is the Internet really is at the heart of the problem while at the same time the Internet will be part of the solution. The Internet only gave legs to a host of crazy and not so ethical ways of doing business which were underlying and were in actuality an underground economy. The Internet brought the underground above ground and placed it out in the open for everyone to see. This underground economy for a large part does not pay taxes which is a detriment to everyone in business.

Unfortunately, because of the low entry level to do business on the Internet everyone and his "uncles, brothers and second cousins" (to quote a popular commercial of the day) can join in this new way of doing business. The bold statement above about ruining any business anytime is exactly true. And you don't have to be a millionaire to make it happen on a smaller scale.

In the coming pages we will detail exactly how the Internet drastically changed the business paradigm and we'll place examples before you which are undeniable. We will also explore how the enemies of capitalism and the western way of life could and might very well exploit this very economic way of doing things to make it so these world economies will never rise again. And we will also explore the possible solutions.

As it stands now, if this author and many economists and experts are to be believed, the end of the pre-2000 world economy has occurred and never will return. It cannot return because of the way the Internet has opened the doors to the new economy. That is unless some very drastic, draconian and dare we say unwanted changes take place. Then, and only then, will it be possible to return the world economy to a true market economy and not the destructive market economy the Internet has created.

The entire premise of this book is not to show where we came from and how we got to where we are going. This of course must be a part of this book if nothing else but to show we have some credibility in this field. The full basis of the book will be to take a very simple premise which has been used for years and to apply this to the world economy itself in a much bigger way. It is what the Internet has done and will continue to do if changes are not made and made quickly.

Everyone from the politicians in Washington to your own state house, to the banker in your local community to the folks at the large investment banks will tell you about the folks on Main Street versus the people on Wall Street. The politicians constantly campaign and use all kinds of rhetoric to explain they know the difference. The truth is very few of them do know the difference between the two.

Wall Street really deals with anyone who has a portfolio which includes stocks and bonds and has the ability to actually purchase stocks at the beginning of an IPO (Initial Public Offering). Main Street is everyone else. That is pretty simplified but basically it's true.

You and I never had the option to purchase Google for the IPO price of ***$85*** when it opened on that first day of trading. Those who did were insiders, investment bankers, the initial shareholders who formed the company and some of their friends who had what a friend of mine used to say "more money than God." The sale on that day raised $1.67 billion and gave Google a market capitalization of more than $23 billion.

"Don't bother looking at making a killing in the stock market," old Joe in Ventura, California told me back then. "That is for guys with lots of money on Wall Street, not guys like you and me."

Joe was 80 years old then and had seen enough to know what he was talking about. After all he was the first guy I knew who didn't believe the Bush Administration when they said Sadam Hussein had WMD's or Weapons of Mass Destruction. Joe turned out to be right about that as well. Old Joe was a pretty smart cookie. I liked old Joe.

The bottom line is he was right. Very few of us, and very few of the people you know, unless you are one of them, are guys on the real Wall Street. You and I may know guys who work there but very few of you probably ever met Bill Gates or Warren Buffet, let alone can call them your friends. You probably can't even call them acquaintances. If you can, then don't stop reading here. You are only partially to blame for this mess we are in.

In actuality, the target of this Internet barrage is really the folks at the other end of the spectrum. These are the people on Main Street. Folks like you and me. Okay, let me repeat that because at this point you are saying "What in the hell is he saying, what did I do?"

In actuality, the target of this Internet barrage is really the folks at the other end of the spectrum. These are the people on Main Street. Folks like you and me.

That's right, you heard it right, we are mainly to blame. Now I've been a guy on Main Street all my life. My father lived on Main Street, his father lived on Main Street and his father lived on Principali Street. My grandfather came from Italy and while he left the old country his father never did. Principali Street must have been in his home town of Potenza, Italy.

Chances are you and your father and grandfather also lived on Main Street, or Kupia Street in Greece, or Fo Street in Hungary or even Belangrijkste Street in Amsterdam. Most of us came from that kind of Main Street. In other words we came about our money the old fashioned way; we earned it, we didn't inherit it and we never won the lottery, we paid taxes and if we were lucky we owned our own business and retired with a few extra bucks in our pocket after 60 or 70 years.

The idea that "most of us" is part of the equation puts a lot more of us in control of how we make and spend our money. Believe it or not those of us on Main Street move around a lot more money than those guys on Wall Street do, every day of our lives, especially weekends. This puts us in a unique position. It puts us in a position to control the flow of capital around the world. The fact we do it every day in $20 bills rather than $2 million wire transfers (or Internet transfers) doesn't matter. We still control the flow of money, where it goes, where it ends up and whether it eventually stays in our pockets or goes into someone else's pockets. It is a matter of fact.

So where am I going with this you ask? You thought this was about the Internet. It is. In the days before say 1992 you cashed your paycheck, put some cash into your pocket and went to the grocery store to buy food for the week. You probably wrote a check to Vons, Albertsons, Safeway or the A&P. You showed them your ID in the form of a credit card and your driver's license. Then you went home and unloaded the groceries from the car.

Next you sat down at the dinner table after having had a meal with the family and while the wife was washing the dishes you got out your checkbook and a stack of bills. You then proceeded with your calculator to figure out how much money you had put in the bank from your payckeck and what your current bills added up to.

If you were lucky you paid all the current bills and looked at your paycheck and there was a balance. You possibly had some pre-tax money, say $100 or so, taken out of your paycheck before you got it for that 401k or Roth IRA. You were building a nice little retirement fund.

If you were not so lucky, like a lot of us, you paid the bills and while you still had three bills to pay you only had a balance of $15.32. Your three bills added up to $121.45. You then either put the bills off until the next paycheck, until you got a windfall from the garage sale you were going to do on Saturday or collected that $100 from your buddy who owed it to you from six weeks ago, or you pulled it out of your savings if you had one. Or you wrote the check figuring "what the heck" I'll "Float" the check hoping I will get some money before the bank cashes it in four to five days. Maybe I win some lotto dough. Or as with most of us you probably just held it off until next pay day and went through the same thing all over again.

At the end of the year you were probably behind a couple thousand bucks, spending more on your credit cards and wondering where it was all going to end. By now the wife had taken a part time job which was starting to look more like full time and you were going out to lunch less often and buying more lotto tickets. It was getting pretty boring, but you knew at least where you stood. This was life around the country for a lot of folks. This was life before the Internet.

Then came the era around 2008. If you were in the "lucky" category things were good. If not, by now you have probably sold your home or lost it, taken everything out of your savings and are just skimming by. Some of you are divorced and some of you are probably still doing just fine. Those of you doing just fine made some good choices and got lucky.

Today? Today you get direct deposit from work so you never see a paycheck. You simply go to the store the day it's deposited and whip out your "Debit" card and pay for the stuff. You figure you need an extra $20 to tide you over for a couple days so you can have "some" cash in your pocket so you get $20 "over" what your purchase was, from the ATM.

Checks? What are they? Can you believe that in 2010, a 19 year old person has probably never written a check in his life and never will? Ask any 19 year old if he has ever cashed a check and they will probably look at you like you are crazy. They've gotten Gift Cards, Pre-Paid Credit Cards, Credit cards and ATM Debit cards but never wrote a check in their life.

Next you will go home and have dinner with the family. After dinner you will go to your office, or your bedroom (wherever you keep your computer) go to your on-line billpay with your bank or to the web sites of your creditors and "click" away the bills until you have paid them all or have nothing left to pay them with.

The words "float a check" never enter your mind. Banks now give you the money from your employer today and take it away tonight. It is simple and quite frankly a very easy and positive way of doing business. It saves a lot of trees in the process too so it really is a nice easy and simple system.

Cash? What's that? Chances are in today's world if you carry any cash it's either a $20 bill or a $100 bill. Seriously when was the last time you reached into your pocket and pulled out $3 in singles or a $5 or $10 bill? You get $20's from the ATM and if you have a need for cash from your bank it's usually in $100 Benjie's. You received ones, fives and tens when you cashed a check. You don't do that anymore.

Okay so we've seen the advances the Internet gave us as really good things, sort of. "Managing" your money by actually looking at it in your hand or feeling a greenback does help you learn how to really manage your money. Someone who has only used ATM and Credit Cards all their life can't comprehend how to manage their money because their money is just a number on a piece of paper. It's not real. They don't touch it, they don't feel it and they certainly can't appreciate it when it is gone. The Internet has done away with our money. We are now just like Buffet and

Gates. We move it around via transfer. We just do smaller amounts of it although there are more of us doing it daily.

The good thing about all of this is first; security, second; ease of use. The first is obvious because you will feel really safe about not getting robbed of your hard earned cash. Of course that is if you don't put your PIN (Personal Identifacation Number) on a piece of paper in your wallet in case you forget it. If you do then any card in your wallet including your Debit, Credit and Pharmacy Cards are the property of anyone who might steal your wallet. All they need is your four digit PIN and they will clean you out of everything you own.

"The Internet makes it easier to steal," Dr. Tim Richardson of Seneca College told me. Richardson teaches Internet business at both Seneca and at the University of Toronto in Canada.

"Let me put it this way, 30 years ago if I were going to rob you it would depend on how many $20 bills you had in your wallet. I might get $60 or $80. Today if I rob you and get your debit card I can take every dollar you have right out of your bank account. I can get as much as possible."

Then of course having it and everything you own accessible to you right on the Internet is a really safe way of doing things too. It should be able to keep you safe from all those friends of yours who want you to share in their millions in Nigeria. The Russian women who want to send you money are really safe folks and then there is that MBA Program, Insurance Pricing and all the other Spam/Scams on the Internet which bombard you daily looking to take away your hard earned money.

"I know it's a scam and I took it to the police when the Russian woman said she was sending me $3000 in a check only if I'd send her $1500 when I cashed it," said Gary in Palmdale, CA. "I know some of the checks are no good but I had a friend say he cashed one and it was good and he kept his share of the money, really."

Huh, huh. Bridges in Brooklyn sound like better deals than we see on the Internet on a daily basis.

While the Internet has opened up tremdenous possiblities Richardson says it changed the way we do business. He points out we are still in the early stages of the World Wide Web, calling it really the intermediate stage and we have yet to touch the tip of the iceberg as to where the Internet will take us. It will always be buyer be ware.

"There are a lot of false prophets out there," he said in regards to the changing business model. "There are a whole bunch of people out there doing it for free."

Dr. Richardson points to the porn industry, considered one of the booming growth industries on the Internet. He says everyone thinks the porn guys are making millions of dollars. Not true because so many are giving it away for free. One might say they are whoring it out. Eventually if a buyer continues to go deeper into the porn site he/she may spend a few dollars on the download or a CD but even that comes at a ridiculously low price. The rub comes when the site has your credit card number, you get scammed and who wants to let their friends know they got scammed by an Internet porn site?

Or worse yet, they get you on the "Free Trial" where you have to put your credit card number on the site. The first month is free. If you don't like what you saw then call and cancel after 30 days, but if you liked it you don't have to do anything again. They will just charge your credit card monthly forever or until you call. At the end of 30 days they are betting you forgot and they keep charging maybe for years because while you don't like the site it's out of sight and out of mind. That $4.99 charge on your credit card for some non-porn name (it will probably read *King Enterprises* instead of *BJ Annie*) is one you usually miss each month when you check your statements. If you are like most folks you miss it because you DON'T check your statements monthly. Before you know it you and thousands of others have spent hundreds of dollars and more for something you don't want and never use. The Internet at its worst.

Think of it this way; the problem with the Internet privacy issue is yes the servers are going after the bad guys on a daily basis and breaking their codes and thwarting them. They are doing a really good job. It is just not good enough. If they were doing such a really good job why do we get new Spam/Scams on a daily basis? Why do Microsoft and the others provide free patches and updates every day? It is because they cannot keep up with the bad guys and they never will. And the worst thing is some of the bad guys don't even make any money at this. They just do it for the heck of it, or worse yet, to show the companies like Microsoft how vulnerable companies like Microsoft really are.

Think of it this way. They are hacking your computer for fun just because they can! And it's never, ever going to stop. As long as you have a computer and do something, anything on-line you will always be fighting the bad guys on a constant basis. The reason is the entry level to be a bad guy and do bad things on the Internet is so low. In fact, it costs nothing to get started.

I've said all of this to say the following; It is easy to be bad on the Internet because, like the title of the book says there is "no barrier to entry" to the Internet. Now let's proceed on this very premise.

Stupid Business; Baseball Cards 101

I began my life in the baseball card and memorabilia business in earnest in 1990. Oh, I had been in the business since I bought my first pack of cards in 1959 I guess. I sold my first collection in 1983 and bought my first collection a few months later. I was hooked. In 1990 my 13 year-old son and I set up at our first neighborhood trade show selling cards from behind an 8-foot table. My cards. It was all my own stuff. Sales that day were over $1000. I was *really* hooked.

The next week we set up at another show. Our total income that day was $18. What happened? The first show I got cherry picked. All my good stuff sold and being new to the business I figured I'd do another $1000 this week. The $18 was a rude awakening. It did not deter me. A few years later I was the Director of Hobby Sales and Media Relations for The Score Board, a trading card maker and memorabilia company in New Jersey. On September 15, 1996 I opened my own card shop in Ventura, California. KC Kings Sportscards was a good store. We ran it like a retail business should be run.

Along the way I published and sold The Brill Report. At first in 1994 it was a paid Fax Newsletter. In our first year working out of my bedroom we did over $30,000. We were on pace to do $50,000 the second year.

I was faced with a tough decision. I really needed to hire someone. A new employee would mean opening an office and moving out of my bedroom. Both were not feasible financially and I wasn't in a position to borrow money for a small business.

Fortunately, sort of, an offer came from Mike Berkus who was a Vice President at The Score Board. He wanted me to come to work there and of course doing that meant I'd have to give up my newsletter. This was somewhat difficult because of the reputation I'd built up with The Brill Report (TBR). This was the first journalistic publication in the industry which was tailored to hard news. All the other publications were what I like to call "rah rah hobby" and stroking the manufacturers because they sold advertising. I did not.

TBR was a subscription based publication based on the hard news principles I'd learned in my time at United Press International and in my broadcast news career which began in 1972. Giving up the only investigative journal in an industry to work for a manufacturer was a difficult choice for me ethically. The offer from TSB was $75,000 a year. I had never made that much before but there still was one question left. Why did TSB want me?

"You guys have a terrible reputation and I have a good one," I told Berkus and CEO Ken Goldin frankly in Goldin's Cherry Hill, New Jersey office that day. "Why do you want me?"

Berkus looked at Goldin and looked back at me.

"You are right, we are trying to change our reputation and bringing guys like yourself and some of the others we've brought in such as Tom Giedeman (another industry positive) shows we're serious about that," Berkus answered.

I swallowed the line and took the money. In five months my firing would be the talk of the industry at the Major League Baseball Fan Fest in Dallas where I went to represent the company. The bizarre thing was they fired me eight days after I moved my family from Los Angeles to New Jersey.

When I tried to pin Berkus down on why he let me go, he couldn't answer.

"You want a reason why we're letting you go?" He asked. "Quite frankly I can't give you one, you didn't do anything wrong."

They did screw me out of my last two weeks pay and when I confronted Goldin with it later on he said he was the one who wanted me gone. He didn't feel like paying $75,000 a year for a Public Relations guy and my distributor sales went from number one in the company to the bottom of our staff.

The fact of the matter was Berkus told me several weeks previously to concentrate on the PR side of the job and to hand all my distributors (whom I was selling to every month) over to my assistant Don, which I did.

"So you feel Berkus set you up?" Asked Goldin. "I didn't know he did that. All I saw were your weekly sales reports and Don had almost all the sales. Oh well."

Goldin's offer to make it up to me was to give me 2500 shares of the company stock which was dying on the vine and never recovered. He gave it to me at $4 a share and it was already down below $3 at the time. The company finally went under but before it did I got a measure of satisfaction.

The CEO of an emerging Collectible Phone Card company, called me several weeks after I was dismissed at TSB. Larry Brilliant's conversation with me went this way….

Larry: "Bob I finally tracked you down, I didn't know you left Score Board."

Bob: "Yes Larry I got fired from there several weeks ago, how did you find me?"

Larry: "Well I called to talk to you and they put me through to Ken Goldin's office. He and Mike Berkus were on the speaker phone with me and I asked 'where is Bob Brill?' They said you were no longer with them and when I asked why, they gave me an answer I think you will like. They said 'well Bob is a religious guy and has ethics and that doesn't fit in with our company.'"

I almost cried. If I would have died that day and they put that on my tombstone I'd have died a happy man. What the firing did do was to send me into the consulting business. I ran a consulting firm for small trading card manufacturers and worked with some of the best people in the industry. Art West and Bill King of "Finish Line Racing" and Dr. Brian Price of Parkhurst were just three of the really good people I worked with. There were some as well who turned out to be more like the head team at Score Board and those relationships I'm glad to say were over quickly.

All of this took place long before every company had a web site and you could buy directly from manufacturers at discounted rates on the Internet. This was in the day of the changing industry of trading cards and memorabilia and after the bubble had burst. What I did learn firsthand from the top down was how screwed up this industry was on the economics side. It is this very screwed up way of doing business which has been exacerbated by the Internet, which lent itself to the ruination of the economy, not only in this country but the world.

Most dealers who dealt in baseball cards had one goal when they set up at a trading card show to sell their wares. Leave with nothing, zero, zip was the name of the game. If you brought 500 cards to sell your goal was to leave with zero cards and somebody else's money in your pocket. That was how success was measured. You walked out empty handed and with a wad of cash. It didn't matter what the economics were and how you got there. Your goal was zero inventories and a wad of cash. In many cases it remains this way even today.

The common conversation of the day at the end of a show when everyone was packing up to leave went like this…

Dealer A: (Holding out a wad of cash) Look at this man, I made $300 today.

Dealer B: Really you *made* $300?

Dealer A: Yeah, I made $300.

Dealer B: You mean you sold $300.

Dealer A: Yes I made $300 selling my cards today.

Dealer B: Okay, you say you made $300. How much did those cards cost you that you sold?

Dealer A: $273

Dealer B: How much did the table cost you here at the show?

Dealer A: $25

Dealer B: How much gas did it cost you to get here in your car?

Dealer A: Oh about $12

Dealer B: And did you eat anything?

Dealer A: Sure, I had a couple of hot dogs, three Coke's and a couple of bags of chips, oh and my kid who helped me had a dog and a coke.

Dealer B: What did that cost you?

Dealer A: Let's see, $11.

Dealer B: Did you pay your kid?

Dealer A: Sure, I gave him $10 for helping me

Dealer B: Those signs you made for the table and the stickers, what did all that cost you?

Dealer A: About $3

Dealer B: So let's see, let me add all this up. It comes to $334. So you lost $34 you didn't make $300.

Dealer A: Like I said I made $300, see I've got it in my hand right here. How much do you want for those 5 boxes of Topps cards on your table before you put them away?

Dealer B: $25 a box.

Dealer A: Will you take $100 for all five? If so I'll take them. I need some more stuff to sell at the next show.

Dealer B: Done deal.

Dealer B had only paid $13 a box for the boxes so he walked out with a profit of $35 on that deal. Dealer A not only lost money, despite his garish arithmetic, he was now into some new product at above a wholesale price and which if at the end of the next show he would probably sell for $18 a box just to make sure he sold them and left with no inventory.

This was how the baseball card industry worked. It wasn't only at the retail level either. The wholesalers were just as bad when it came to their business practices. The typical wholesale guy would buy his maximum of every product direct from the manufacture if he had a direct account. These were tough to get until about 1994. Post 1993 the card makers were giving them away like candy. Some were even begging you to take them.

The wholesaler would mark most products up five-to-10 percent on average. If he didn't sell it all to his dealers and store owners in a day or two he'd drop the price hoping just to get rid of it. In many cases he'd sell it for less than he paid for it just to have enough money to pay for the next product coming down the line.

The idea was if he dumped it quickly enough he wouldn't get hurt too badly. Then when a suspected hot product came out, a real winner, he'd jack up the wholesale price to 25 or even 50 percent above his cost instead of the five-10 percent he charged on the normal products. The idea was you would make enough on the winners to make it all worthwhile. There were some winners too. There were more losers which is why when the companies saw things really declining in late 1991 and forward they started cranking out more and more lines of products.

In 1990 Emmitt Smith of the Dallas Cowboys had three rookie cards. The most sought after card was usually the rookie (RC) or first card of a player. In 1993 Drew Bledsoe had over 60 different first year cards as a rookie! The problem was, as I learned at The Score Board, the only time a manufacturer has income to keep his company alive and pay bills and employees is when he ships a card product. The rest of the time he's making the product and building it and soliciting it. When he ships he gets money so the only way to get more money is to ship more products.

These items were designed as collectibles. They were sold as collectibles. They were in reality widgets. By 1997 the industry had nearly totally collapsed and the few manufacturers which were left began to try to figure out how they could keep people coming into the dwindling number of hobby stores.

When I was at Score Board we had a list of over 3000 trading card stores around the country. There were 800 private dealers in Los Angeles alone. By 2010 the number had dwindled to the hundreds and few of those were pure sports card stores. They were selling everything from memorabilia to coins to plush stuffed animals to stay alive and most had converted to gaming products such as Pokemon and Magic the Gathering.

The card industry had imploded on itself and tried everything from Internet gaming to selling Lacrosse cards to get back in the game. Upper Deck, one of the three remaining mainstream card dealers lost the bulk of its licenses and even got caught printing counterfeit gaming cards. Topps, purchased and taken private by former Disney kingpin Michael Eisner, focused on what it had left as core products; baseball and football. Panini, the Italian sticker maker, bought up the company which owned the Donruss brands and ended up in the early 2000's with more professional licenses than the other companies combined.

The card industry was virtually destroyed by many factors including greed, but the economic structure of the industry, especially at the dealer level preceded the Internet. When the Internet arrived it made it that much easier to continue and move this way of doing business into the mainstream. It literally obliterated the line between wholesale and retail. The line vanished when the Internet arrived because it made it very easy for the average person to do exactly what store owners were doing.

The introduction of eBay took the matter to unbelievable heights and continued to bring the economics of the industry to the depths no one ever thought could happen. The Internet website eBay did bring more "collectors" into the market place. It did so as to destroy any real profit margins store owners and dealers could get.

It can be argued more product was being moved because of eBay since a store owner in California could easily sell items to a collector in Florida and vice-versa. Sometimes at inflated margins if the product was right. Some would call this the essence of a true market economy. In the long run and not many years after this began however things started to change drastically and eBay was no longer the booming sales driver it once was. Dealers were getting killed and stores began to fade away.

The home office had replaced the hobby store. Dealers decided the cost of running a legitimate retail operation, a store front, was no longer viable. Walk-in traffic had slowed to a crawl because people were not shopping at a store which needed to keep prices at proper levels so the rent could be paid and the dealers make a living. They just went on-line to buy a box of cards from some guy for $53, when the store owner was selling it for $69. The problem was they both paid $50 for the product from the manufacturer or their wholesaler. The line between wholesale and retail was gone. Why own a store?

The problem became worse as more industries faced the same situation. For all its greatness eBay became the killer of mom and pop retail stores. The American Dream of owning a business and running it yourself with your wife and kids was history. As the economy turned sour in the early 2000's it got even worse. Fewer people were opening small businesses because their customers could always find it cheaper on the Internet. If not on eBay, then on some wholesaler's website.

The guys who were known as distributors and wholesalers were now selling directly to the public at the same price they used to sell to their stores. Now it was just easier to sell directly to the consumer instead of going through the middleman or the retail outlet. It took awhile but even the giants such as Target, Wal-Mart and Sears were affected by this change. Even Topps was selling its hot selling sealed factory sets directly to the public via its website. At least Topps was selling with what it considered a normal margin. Topps always considered 35-percent a normal margin, not the standard retail margin of 50-percent. So it really did hurt their retailers.

Blockbuster Video began closing stores because NetFlix sold directly to the customer via downloads. DVD's had replaced VHS and DVD's were replaced by the computer download via the Internet. Movies were being sold for pennies on the dollar because it cost virtually nothing to sell them on the Internet.

The in-turn effect? Few people were going out to movies so the price jumped from $8 to $10 to $15 and more to see a movie in the theatre. With fewer movies being made by studios, since so many were being made independently and put on-line, the big studios were facing huge financial problems of their own. They were becoming obsolete. Who would risk millions to make a movie when someone would make it for pennies on the dollar with decent equipment and put it on the Internet for nothing?

They would reap no profit but they would "get their name out there" and hope to make big bucks on their reputation. Unfortunately, where they wanted to go changed because of the way they did business and the end result was the place they wanted to go; the big studio was gone. It was put out of business by the Internet movie makers.

If you wonder why you see so many remakes of old movies the reason is simple. Figures show when you remake a film which was a hit you have a 60-percent built-in audience who saw the film and now are willing to pay to see the new version. Remakes such as "True Grit" and "Footloose" made huge profits for the studios. With 60-percent built-in at inflated prices you don't have to have many newer folks who never saw the old film (they probably weren't even born when the original was released) to bring in enough money to make a profit.

Heads of studios don't take risks anymore. If it's a remake it is gold, if it is a blockbuster with lots of computer graphics building the characters you are really only paying actors to talk not act. Big budget, high concept films, remakes and animated films are not risky or at least not nearly as risky as a well written drama people love to see but usually don't pay for anymore.

The other part of the equation is a film has a very short life in theaters. A few weeks after it is released at the box office it's available on DVD or better yet streaming on your computer. You of course can hook your computer up to your big screen and watch it all day long. Studios control those releases and make their extra money there. No risk.

The Internet is responsible for a huge part of this and the reason why is there is no barrier to entry in doing business on the

Internet. It is too easy, too inexpensive and in the end the hand destroys the mouth which feeds it.

The bottom line in all of this is there must be profit margins in every business and those profit margins must be designed to keep the business in business, make a profit for the owner with enough to make a living and to provide enough capital to create new jobs and expansion. Business on the Internet is designed to do exactly the opposite.

Internet business is designed to deliver the product from the manufacturer in the cheapest possible way at the cheapest possible price. This occurs even at the risk of losing money to make the sale. The latter is called predatory pricing and is illegal on the brick and mortar front. Try stopping it on the Internet. You can't.

Predatory Pricing

By definition Predatory Pricing is basically when a company purposely sells its products below the competition in order to drive the competition out of business, and in doing so actually loses money when making its own sales. In other words company A is willing to lose money selling its products so cheaply in order to drive company B out of business. Presumably then when company B is no longer in business company A will be the only company left standing and can sell its products at whatever price it wants including vastly inflated prices. This is the real idea behind predatory pricing. It is also a monopoly which is illegal in the United States.

Difficult to prove but it is still illegal in the United States, under federal law, and in several countries around the globe including France, Germany and Australia. Wal-Mart, the biggest retailer in America, has been accused many times of using this tactic including not only the USA but in Germany. In Canada the law is *Canada, Section 50(1)(c) of the Competition Act*.

In a Federal Trade Commission Report issued January 29, 2004, regarding a letter from the Alabama Legislature the law was defined per the US Supreme Court and its key decision on the law.

"The Supreme Court has directly addressed low-pricing strategies. In *Brooke Group v. Brown & Williamson Tobacco Corp.*, the leading case in this area, the Court expressly held that a defendant does not violate the federal antitrust laws by cutting prices merely because the low prices decrease a competitor's profits. "Low prices benefit consumers regardless of how those prices are set. . . . To hold that the antitrust laws protect competitors from the loss of profits due to such price competition would, in effect, render illegal any decision by a firm to cut prices in order to increase market share." To be unlawful, the low prices must, at a minimum, be predatory. "[S]o long as they are above predatory levels, [low prices] do not threaten competition . . . We have adhered to this principle regardless of the type of antitrust claim involved."

The Court has defined predatory pricing, in turn, as "pricing below an appropriate measure of [the defendant's] cost for the purpose of eliminating competitors in the short run and reducing competition in the long run." Although the Court has not stated what the appropriate measure of cost should be, prominent antitrust scholars and several federal circuit courts have concluded that the price-cutter's marginal costs, or a close proxy such as average variable costs, should be the yardstick. "

The bottom line is the fact Predatory Pricing (herein called PP) is very difficult to prove because companies do have sales in order to best the competition. They should not have sales to drive the competition unfairly out of business.

However, trying to enforce this issue on the Internet is impossible and nowhere is it really addressed as being illegal. The Internet remains the Wild West and predatory pricing is evident everywhere especially on eBay. Although it must be said the "intent" in many cases is not there on any large scale to the average person. Look around and you will see many examples of it on lots of websites around the globe.

So how does one drive the competition out of business by using PP on the Internet? The previous example of the "porn" industry is a realistic one. Give it away for free. Here is a simple example of this theory of doing business and why it works on the surface but in reality is a destroyer of business overall.

One of the ways to make money with a website is to sell advertising. What attracts advertisers to a web site is the number of hits and the number of unique users. Unique users are people who come to the site for a unique experience and don't just click on it and float around the site. They are people who, for want of a better description, came to the site to check it out and spend some time. The more unique users means the more attention your site is drawing from potential customers. Porn sites get a lot of unique users as opposed to say a news article site.

Hot columnists get lots of unique users. Sites on the news site Examiner.com for instance vary widely. Articles from one Examiner doing stories about international news don't get nearly as many unique users as a site on NASCAR tidbits or Hollywood gossip. People just keep returning to the latter sites on a daily basis and may go there several times a day.

These latter sites are where advertisers want to place their ads and often will pay dearly to have their name linked to the site or on the site in a display banner ad. If it costs nothing to go to the site and enter its pages the more viewers are likely to return to the site and cruise around its pages many, many times. Charge to read the site and Internet users have a tendency to back off. They can get the information somewhere else on the Web for free, so why go to your site?

Advertisers see two very similar sites on the Web. Site A charges $1.99 for its service and gets 100 hits a day. Site B offers its service for free and gets 1000 hits a day. Which one is the advertiser more likely to want to be on? It is obvious Site B with ten times the viewers is going to draw the attention of the advertiser and his advertising dollars. Site A may have been a more legitimate business and still gets advertisers but Site B by doing business on its site for free has gained money from potential advertisers.

Soon Site A will see the vast majority of its users flock to Site B for many reasons. It is free, it now offers more content with lots of advertisers who in turn are giving away deals to draw attention to their business and it is getting more "comments" from viewers because simply it has more viewers. Soon Site A will either be forced to alter its business model and go "free" or just plain go out of business. Site B wins by doing business in a very stupid manner.

The owner of Site B might counter with if "I'm so stupid how come I am the one left doing business?" Doing business and being in business are two different things and while Site B may be the last one standing, staying in business and making money, making a living, expanding and creating jobs is not in his business plan.

Wal-Mart has been the target of charges of PP in many cases world-wide. Prescription Drugs being a big part of the program in the Upper Midwest. The reason why it doesn't get the anti-consumer reactions is because people see the price to them as being a bargain. Most people would rather save money than see the real problem behind such actions and that is to drive competition out of the business. Competition creates lower prices. Using PP as a means to do it only signifies an ulterior motive such as driving the competition out of business then jacking up the prices to whatever the remaining store wants to charge.

In Minnesota for instance in September, 2007, the Associated Press reported Wal-Mart was forced to raise its prices on certain prescription drugs in that state because of unfair pricing. Minnesota law prohibits companies from selling a product for less than what it costs the company to buy it in the first place. Wal-Mart was forced to raise its price on a certain birth control pill to $26.88 for a one month supply. It was selling it for only $9 in several other states. Nine drugs were affected in the order from Minnesota. Turns out there were nine states which had similar laws at the time. A competitor, Target, realistically could not match the Wal-Mart price while complying with local laws. Wal-Marts response was its drug program had already saved consumers $5.5 million dollars.

It was what could be seen as a clear case of PP and in the end Wal-Mart was forced to stop its unfair practice. This in the end created competition because Target had to respond and lower its prices to where both companies could make a legitimate profit and the public was still served.

In theory, if Wal-Mart were allowed to continue to sell at the $9 level, losing money in the transaction, Target would have been forced out of the game because it would not sell below its cost just to compete with the bigger Wal-Mart. Wal-Mart could afford to take the hit over and over again while Target could not. By law both Target and Wal-Mart were forced to stay in competition, make profits and keep hundreds of workers employed. If Wal-Mart had driven Target out of business in Minnesota jobs would have been lost and Wal-Mart could have raised prices to whatever level it wanted and those consumer discounts would have evaporated. The public would be harmed and Wal-Mart would have been that much richer and more powerful leading to a monopoly. That word is the worst word in the business world and slammed down by the US Supreme Court for well over a century.

The Internet is wide open and to say it is ripe for fraud puts it back 10 years. It is full of fraud.

"The one thing the Internet has done is it's opened it up so small business and consumers can buy goods directly from the Far East now like never before," Said Erik S. Syverson, Los Angeles based Internet lawyer who specializes in Internet law. "So there is a tremendous amount of fraud and the purchasing of counterfeit goods from China and other countries in Asia."

Alibaba.com is commonly referred to as the eBay of China and while eBay made inroads to China as did Yahoo, both were left high and dry by the way China does business. Basically China offers money and access to foreign firms and entrepreneurs with the understanding Intellectual Property (IP) rights remain in China for the most part. The Chinese can do whatever they want with what the foreign company develops because China was willing to put up the money. Alibaba.com is basically the home-grown eBay auction site and if you thought getting satisfaction on eBay has been difficult over the years, try dealing with the Chinese model.

"The Internet has opened up that world and led to an influx of counterfeit goods into America from the Far East," said Syverson. "You don't have to go to downtown LA to find a shady guy on a street corner anymore. You can go directly to Alibaba.com from the comfort of your own home and click."

Predatory Pricing is rampant on the Internet but difficult to prove and even more important it is not really against any existing laws which matter. Not every country has a rule against it and how do you enforce such rules if they did? More to come on that later in this book.

Syverson says the Information Super Highway has become Ripoff Road.

"People come to me all the time and say they bought Garman GPS watches on Alibaba.com dirt cheap and they either never got them or they were counterfeit. And I say 'of course they are counterfeit what did you expect?'"

Syverson says China is a major problem when it comes to Internet fraud.

"As far as goods and predatory pricing and counterfeit goods we see the Internet has opened those channels tremendously. People are so hungry to do business with anything attached to China they are getting ripped of by sellers of supposed brand name products at discount rates and China could care less about IP rights."

It isn't only China and other foreign nations where the problems begin and come home to roost in the United States. Some of it is home-grown. As was mentioned earlier in this book regarding the Porn Web Sites, the Continuity Programs flourish on the Internet. Continuity Programs are an industry term for giving you a one month free trial but you have to have a credit card on file to start the trial. Once they have your credit card they begin charging you a monthly fee in the second month unless you call and cancel. Even then it is difficult to stop the transactions.

"Continuity Programs are the oldest scam in the book and the worst of them all in my opinion is the Video Professor," added Syverson. "And he's back on."

The Video Professor was fined by the Federal Government for duping people into thinking they were getting hundreds of "Free" videos when they were actually charging their credit cards.

The problem was if you called to cancel it almost took an Act of God to get through to them and cancel the program

Then John Scherer, aka The Video Professor, even went on to sue a hundred folks who posted challenges to his product on web sites. Nate Anderson's Law and Order blog posted this one;

"I had purchased one piece of software from Video Professor... before I knew what was happening, my credit card was overdrawn and more attempted charges were constantly occurring. I kept calling customer service, returned the original software and heard many promises of the 100 percent refund, less S/H. This has been over 3 years now." –Tina.

So where is the Video Professor now? On-line at the video professor website.

The bottom line is once again the business model has changed. What you can't legally do in the real world can be duplicated, legally, in the virtual world. Basically not many laws do exist to protect businesses and consumers in the virtual world of the Internet.

"To the extent there is law it favors the web sites and the web site operators," said Syverson. "At the Federal level we don't have a heck of a lot of regulation. Some copyright and trademark specific laws but other than that we're pretty light on Internet specific language."

There are reasons for leaving the Internet the Wild West as it is now. Regulations might have killed the many advances which have been made in the name of the Internet. As Dr. Richardson said previously we are only in the beginning stages. Syverson agrees.

"Consider it like the auto industry. Think of it in 1925 and where it was in 1965 and 85 and 2000. Where was television in 1960 and where is it now? It may be replaced by Google with content provided by anybody and everybody."

Commercial television, radio and of course newspapers are really in danger with the Internet. Newspapers have all but gone away and if not totally they are heavily supplemented on-line and for Free. The Wall Street Journal has tried going the on-line subscription route with mixed results.

Everyone who has studied the Internet and its effects knows about the slow death the print industry is dying. Newspapers are drying up and while some publications have adapted such as magazines, they may just be a few years away from being eliminated and jobs with them.

"Some industries have adapted such as magazines and newspapers but those two will never be able to make the money on the internet they are hoping," pointed out Dr. Pamela Falk a distinguished lecturer who teaches international economics and United Nations Studies at Hunter College in New York. "They have launched their Internet version but they are still relying on subscriptions and paper and those are having a tough time keeping their budgets balanced."

A recent poll indicated a large number of Americans would not really be affected one way or the other should their local newspaper fold up and go away. Many just feel they will get their news on-line. This begs the question, if the newspaper goes and employees go with it, who will write the news for consumers to read on-line? Bloggers are not reporters in the context of reporting factual hard-core news.

"The Brill Report," this writer's own publication was a money-maker as a Fax Newsletter in the mid 1990's. Brought back as an on-line subscription newsletter post 2000 it was highly respected but had fewer subscribers. One letter we got stated "Why would I pay for this information?" He was partially right. Much of the information was available elsewhere by "searching" the Internet for free. Some of it was exclusive to The Brill Report.

Eventually TBR moved to a free on-line content provider. It lasted for about a year and even though readership jumped substantially it was not enough to attract advertisers. To continue doing it for free was what you might call "cost prohibitive." The publication has ceased to appear. The bottom line is there was no money in it to support it.

Commercial radio is battling with what to do about the Internet and as Syverson stated commercial television is in the same straights. Both, from the major corporate level, are trying to cut costs by soliciting viewers to send in their video and audio on demand for free, for the joy of seeing their video on television or their voice on radio. Radio reporters are being forced to carry video equipment on the job for no extra pay. The pitch is "what do we need you for when viewers and listeners can provide content for free?"

Predatory pricing? It is certainly is. Harming one industry to make money by undercutting costs. With the Internet and the lack of laws and controls it may be the only way commercial television and radio as well as print journals can survive. If you are reading this book on a Kindle you will understand fully.

"With the internet you are damned if you do and damned if you don't," Syverson points out. "One of the things people like so much about the Internet and why it has developed so rapidly is the lack of regulation. The other side of the coin though is there are a lot of people who are harmed in many ways."

And as Professor Richardson has stated, it has only just begun.

Real Cost of Doing Business on the Internet

This book has stated there is no barrier to doing business on the Internet. The title "No Barrier" proclaims it. One man in the know recently told me of course there is a barrier to doing business on the Internet; computers, search engine optimization, web site maintenance and more. To which we say "Baloney."

It is so cheap to do business on the Internet, even if you do it the most expensive way, there really is very little barrier to entry which equates to no barrier. Let us look at the simple rules for doing business in real life versus the virtual world.

We will start with a very simple business to get into, which also translates well to the Internet. We can select any number of businesses for which the following scenario will work but we are picking a very simple one which any average Joe on the street may like to begin his commercial venture.

We have selected the sports card and memorabilia industry because it is a very simple business to get into on any level. You don't need a lot of expertise if you have any understanding of retail business at all. Sure there are some industry specific things but to be sure they can be learned quickly and on the job.

It is not unlike starting a clothing store, a furniture store, a crafts shop, or for that matter a small restaurant, a bicycle shop or even some services which also sell retail products. For terms of the Internet it might not even be too different from insurance and real estate brokers with the exception of the required licensing and schooling.

Let us start our card store in Ventura, California, about 60 miles from Los Angeles. This is a community of about 100,000 people, a metro area of about 250,000. Sounds like a reasonable place to start a new retail business.

Joe, we'll call our business man, Joe. Joe is 45 years old, has a few credit cards with about $10,000 in credit available. He wants to open a store in a place with a decent amount of walk in traffic. The best place is a real regional mall, or at least it used to be, but he cannot afford the rent there or the length of the lease. He's not sure he can survive the first year in business. Statistics show probably about 50-percent of all new businesses fail in the first year. According to the US Small Business Administration 95-percent will fail to last five years. The cost of renting in a mall with all the mall rules and regulations is too much for our Joe.

He finds a nice strip mall with about a half dozen other firms. There is a Chinese Restaurant, a bakery, an Italian eatery, a grocery store, a Laundromat and a Florist. Starbucks and McDonalds are within sight and a Pizza Parlor is across the street. Parking is good and a school is about three blocks away.

"This is perfect, just perfect," Joe tells his wife Sue, who is skeptical about his business plans but goes along anyway. "We have parking, food, families, a school so what more could I ask for?"

And there is a vacancy. Joe sees the sign "For Lease" in front of what looks to be a 2,000 square foot store front. He grabs his cell phone and calls the number. A broker answers and says he'll be right over. Within 15 minutes the broker, Bill arrives and he opens the door for Joe and Sue.

Joe begins imagining where he'll put the showcases for the cards, the wall racks for the boxes; he sees lots of memorabilia hanging on the wall. Some of this he already has because he has decided if he gets into this business he's no longer a collector. He realizes, very smartly he cannot do both.

"So what are we talking about here Bill, what is this going to cost me to put in a baseball card store?" Joe asks.

Bill hesitates and wonders if he really wants to rent to a baseball card store owner and starts to ask questions. Bill realizes Joe is a smart guy with little experience at running a shop but is impressed by his business plan and his determination.

"Well it rents for $1.25 a square foot and at 2000 square feet that comes out to $2500 a month plus triple net," Bill answers.

Joe and Sue look at Bill with surprise. Not so much at the price which is more than they want to pay, but what the heck is triple net?

"A triple net lease is a type of commercial leasing agreement," Bill answers realizing their question before it's asked. "In a triple net lease, you pay taxes, insurance, and maintenance in addition to the rent."

Bill explains this is pretty standard in renting a mall or strip mall space. A stand alone building may not offer this type of rent but in the end all the businesses in the complex share this cost. Bill explains the triple net for this unit is another $500 per month bringing the monthly rent to $3000 with a five percent leeway or increase each year of the five year lease.

"That is another thing, we are a new business and well quite frankly I would rather not have a five year lease," Joe says.

Bill says he understands and while his owner would be against it, he has the authority to grant a three year lease with a six month option out. In other words if Bill gives him six months notice at the end of two and a half years, he can be out at the end of three years. Otherwise it must be five years.

Joe and Sue agree to rent the place. They must come up with the first and last months' rent and a $1000 deposit which is refundable if the place is very clean when they vacate. It is more than they want to pay but the place is perfect for their needs. It means $7000 out of their pocket of which half goes on a credit card.

Joe and Sue own a home and a friend of theirs, who is a lawyer, said they should incorporate or at least do business as a Limited Liability Company, an LLC in California. This will protect them in case of lawsuits. If they get sued because some kid tripped in their store and hit his head on the corner of a counter leaving him injured for life, their home and life style is protected. Only the business would be lost. This is much better than doing business as a sole proprietor which protects them not at all.

They go on-line to file for their LLC status. It is less than $100 but the LLC annual tax status fee is $800 and must be paid up front. They look into filing for an LLC in Nevada and Delaware where there are no state taxes. They can do this and save the money. Nope. As it turns out if they become a corporation or LLC in another state, California considers them a "foreign corporation" with a foreign corporation fee. The fee? The same $800. They decide to file in California.

The state also requires a State of California Resale License.

"Okay, how much is that going to cost?" Sue asks.

"Oh it's free," says the clerk behind the counter. "We want you to have this because it is how we bill you for your state sales tax."

The city of Ventura is very easy on licensing fees for new businesses. For less than $100 you can go into business and a store such as the one Joe and Sue will open will only cost them less than $100 a year in relicensing. If it were in Los Angeles it would be about $300 a year or more.

Joe would like to sell coins in his store as well but finds out to do that he really needs a license from the state which sort of makes him similar to a pawn shop. He gives up on that idea. Plus there are many more rules and regulations dealing with selling coins over-the-counter and buying them. A major part of the problem is putting them into the state's theft computers and holding the merchandise for 30 days to make sure they are not stolen. No such law on baseball cards.

Joe and Sue are required to have insurance on their business and they go to Farmers, State Farm and many more where they come up with an average price. It is going to cost them $2200 a year for insurance on the business which is required by law. They can make the payments monthly.

After talking to the tenants at the other businesses in the building they learn a couple of other disturbing facts. They will likely pay about $300 a month in electric bills, $65 a month for water and sewage services which is not covered in the triple net. The alarm system with in-store cameras will cost $850 to install and will cost another $40 a month to monitor. Since the front of the unit is all plate glass and card stores are an easy target for "smash and grab" burglaries they must put sliding fencing along the front. It is $1000 per panel and they have two panels. Sue puts another $2000 on the credit card and is getting somewhat worried. They've spent almost $10,000 so far and haven't opened the doors.

They have decided to call the place J&S Sports for Joe and Sue. Sue is a graphics designer by trade and comes up with an idea for the sign. It's simple, sort of a pennant with the J&S flowing with the name Sports in block lettering. It is in three colors which are based on the flag. This means red, white and blue.

Dave of Dave's Signs comes out and gives them the price. To make the sign and place it will be $3500 if the electrical parts are not damaged inside the walls. Luckily they are not. Sue pulls out her second credit card as the first one is maxed out.

The new business couple decides they need a total of 10 showcases for the store plus shelving. They go around to several different retail stores who have recently gone out of business and talk to the owners. New showcases are cost prohibitive. They could cost up to $3000 each. Used ones can be had for $50-$75 each and look just as nice. They find the eight showcases they need at a price of $60 each or $480. A rental truck and a couple guys to help move the cases cost them another $300. Joe reasons it is better to pay some homeless guy to move the showcases than the doctor to work on his back after he injures it lifting stuff he cannot possibly lift.

The shelving Joe finds at Home Depot. He figures out what he needs and lays out another $750. The handy man he hires charges him another $450 to put them up. Office Depot has nice Casio cash registers which aren't too fancy and Sue picks one up for $400 and some other office type supplies such as stickers and pens, and pencils for another $100.

After filing for his new business permit with the county, another $50, they are required to place an advertisement in the local paper stating they are a "new business" concern. The advertisement is required by law. The cost? They choose the cheap $75 option.

Now they go to the phone company. Business lines include one for the fax machine, one for the business, one for the computer and one for the credit card machine. They must take credit cards and they get lots of calls right away.

They settle on a company which charges them $800 for the credit card machine (monthly payments are made) $.50 per debit card transaction and 2.5 percent of each credit card transaction. There is a minimum of $10 per month as a fee versus the 2.5 percent. They will easily exceed the fee but there will be other fees along the way.

The phone company, by the way, charges them $215 per month for the service with a free yellow pages ad and a free Internet ad. If they want a bigger ad with graphics it will cost them more. They don't. They get calls every day about "other" yellow pages and Internet ads.

Joe talks to his local wholesale distributor about products and he learns they have a program where they will give Joe and Sue $500 worth of supplies on consignment to get started as a good will gesture. They will have six months to pay this off but as a new business they must pay for other products as they go for the first year. This means when they pick them up or before they are delivered. Once they are in business for a year they can set up a credit line. If they use their credit card to pay for any purchase the distributor will add 2.5 percent to the transaction because this is what he is charged for taking the card and he works on such small margins he can't afford the "hit."

Joe and Sue agree and take $3000 worth of new products to open the store, the consigned supplies and with the rest of the stuff Joe already has in his own inventory they are ready to open the doors.

Whoops! They forgot the advertising for the new business in the local paper. A grand opening is scheduled and the newspaper suggests a quarter page layout plus they will get a free mention on the paper's website. The cost of the quarter page is $1500 for one time. They choose to spend $1000 on several smaller ads over four days.

Joe and Sue come up with some great promotions including prize giveaways, contests, free pizza and soda. It costs them another $1000 to do all of this including in-kind products. They also hire a friend for the day to help out and pay him $50.

And on that big day they open their new venture! Sales for the first day are $2000. Sales for the first month are about $10,000. Joe and Sue are not happy but they are determined and having only $5000 in reserve cash in the bank they are nervous but they plug on. They are entrepreneurs in the retail trade; better known as Small Business Persons.

To open their business it cost them, in cold hard cash and credit, a grand total of $24, 635. That is the cost of opening a small retail business in a small to medium city in California and the monthly costs continue at a rate of close to $10,000 with rent and utilities being a part of that.

Henry decides to open a baseball card business on the Internet. He'll use eBay and he'll use his own website. Unlike Joe and Sue he's not going to need a retail store front, he's not going to need showcases, insurance, an alarm system, much inventory, a credit card machine, a sign, newspaper advertising, he'll avoid the city tax but will get the state Resale Tax form although he'll fudge what he collects in taxes because he won't even try to collect them except on a limited basis.

He will have to pay the county fee and the newspaper fee to show he is in business but he won't need a phone line, a fax line or yellow pages advertising. He doesn't want local calls because he's not really interested in the local market. No LLC or corporate fees because there is little danger of someone getting hurt in his office at home which is where his business rests.

Henry decides to use a full website through Intuit or one of the other pre-fabricated website companies. It costs him about $60 to $600 a year in hosting fees. He chooses the more expensive option because he gets a shopping cart with it and then joins Constant Contact for an email service to send out his promotions for $15 a month. A web company to maximize his searches is a possibility and at some point might be needed but for now he will hold off on that.

So let's see. Henry already has his computer as does everyone else in the world. Instead of credit cards he'll take PayPal which is basically free except for the 3-percent fee they charge on transactions versus the 2.5 percent and minimum monthly statement Joe and Sue will pay. His inventory is his own and what he buys on line from other dealers via PayPal on eBay or through other networks. He also buys from the same distributor

Joe buys from. The distributor sees no difference in the store front and the Internet dealer who in some cases are selling to the same customers although more of Henry's are out of the area.

So let's see the cost for Henry to set up his business is $780, which is $23, 873 less than Joe and Sue and basically no monthly cost unless he does business. Those costs will be eBay fees and PayPal fees and if he chooses to market through Constant Contact. Even if he chooses to pick up a service to optimize his searches, which is questionable at best anyway, he won't spend more than $500 a month to do that. He probably won't because there are better ways of doing it himself. He'll use Facebook, Twitter and other industry sites to expand his business.

Joe and Sue will eventually be forced into doing many of the same things Henry is doing including eBay and Facebook. All of this will cost them more time and only make them a little more money compared to the hours involved.

Six months after Joe and Sue opened they run into one of their former customers at the Post Office. He hasn't been in for some time and was a good spender. Tommy was spending $750 a week buying an average of seven boxes of sports cards.

"Hey Tommy how's it going, I haven't seen you in some time, where have you been?" Joe asks as he reaches out his hand to shake.

"Oh I've been around," Tommy says shyly.

Joe recognizes something is wrong and Tommy doesn't want to say, so he speaks up.

“Something wrong Tom, did I offend you or something?”

“No it’s not that, it’s just that well, I’ve found someone else cheaper and I mean a lot cheaper, so I’m still buying and while I’d like to buy from you I just can’t when the other guy is so much less expensive,” Tommy explains. “He’s a guy on the Internet here in Ventura.”

Joe is dumbfounded. Tommy goes on to tell him the boxes Joe charges $100 each for, the other guy, Henry sells for $75, which means he can get an average of two more boxes a week from Henry. Joe tries to explain he and Henry (who he has heard of from his distributor) both pay $70 per box for the same products. Since Henry sells out of his home on the Internet he only makes $5 per box and he can do that while Joe and Sue have a business to run and must charge $25 more per box to make a profit, pay the bills and stay in business.

The bottom line for Tommy is more products at a cheaper price. The bottom line for Joe is staying in business; the bottom line for Henry is he could care less. If he makes $5 per box and sells 25 boxes per day that is $125 in his pocket or $600 per week. If Joe and Sue only profited $600 per week they couldn’t even pay the rent for the month and would be out of business. Henry is happy with that, no more local competition.

Cost of doing business on the Internet is really devastatingly low. In other words there is no real barrier to entry.

Real Wealth Versus Real Life

In the beginning of this book we made the statement we could destroy any business at anytime by using the Internet and we did not have to be wealthy to do it. This is correct. However, being wealthy in the first place, or at least well heeled, would be an advantage.

Take for instance the automobile industry. Could a wealthy person, and we're talking billionaire here, not the less than wealthy millionaire, destroy a certain automobile maker if he so chose to do so? The answer is yes but not likely due to the fact the way the industry works. The billionaire could however destroy the network through which those cars are sold; the distributors, the auto dealerships. How? Not unlike the previous scenario dealing with trading cards or other retail outlets.

While the preceding scenario may seem a bit far fetched to some readers it should be emphasized we chose this particular industry for one reason; it is among the most difficult to destroy via the Internet. There are any number of other businesses in the United States which can be destroyed in the manner which follows and much easier. We chose this one because it is so difficult, just to show it is possible.

An automobile dealership purchases a certain amount of new cars from the automaker. General Motors, Ford, Lexus or whomever sells a certain amount of new cars to privately owned dealerships. They each get a certain number of new cars to sell to their customers. Some of these cars are sold long before delivery to well heeled regular customers.

These are customers who don't care about price as much as being the first person to have this new car. They are the premium customers and they are the folks every business caters to and really "takes care of." They are repeat buyers usually and they buy from "Dealership A" because first of all they've been buying from Dealership A for years. Secondly they like the service and the feeling they are being treated well, first class so to speak.

The dealership needs these people because they pay retail usually and strong profits are made. There are other first line people who don't haggle much on the price and these are folks who also buy early and while maybe they don't buy a new car every year they may lease a car for a year or two or purchase one every couple of years. The dealership needs them as well and this is because of the profit margin.

As the year goes on and some of those new cars sit and are still available at the end of the model year the dealership begins discounting the price. The company has made its profit up front and now it just wants to get its money back on the last of the "new" car models. They paid $15,000 and are willing to sell them for $15,000 and take that $15,000 and invest it in next year's models. They sold the first batch for $30,000 each so they made their profit in what's called "up front" or "the front end."

Enter the billionaire who says he has a real hate-hate relationship with a certain manufacturer and he wants to destroy this manufacturer. The way he'll do it is through the dealerships. He can't really hurt the automaker directly but he can hurt him by putting the dealerships out of business.

Let's, for grins say, Dr. Big Stick is a billionaire investor who is flush with cash and he wants to go out and destroy the automaker called FLOOD Cars, Inc. Flood Cars has 100 dealerships around the country which will each get 100 new Flood models for 2011. The direct cost of these new Flood 2011 models is $5,000 each with a resale retail dealership price of $10,000 each. We chose these numbers at random for clarity sake. We understand the prices of new cars vary widely and from day to day.

The billionaire, Mr. Stick, knows if he can arrange to buy about half, maybe more of the new 2011 models he can control the market. He doesn't want to control the market though, he wants to destroy it and in turn destroy the dealerships which in turn will damage the main company, Flood Cars, Inc. Mr. Stick must figure a way to purchase at least 5,000 of the new 2011 models for as close to factory cost as possible. This is $50 million to him.

Through a third party shell company he makes arrangements to purchase a number of these cars from the manufacturer directly. He offers the manufacturer a small percentage over the $5,000 per car which the manufacturer being greedy agrees to. Flood Cars decides to make more money up front by selling a portion to Mr. Stick's shell company, which it doesn't know by the way is owned by Mr. Stick.

Then Mr. Stick starts dealing with the dealers directly. Knowing they will each have a few of the "well heeled" repeat customers to sell to but at the same time will have a lot of other cars to sell to other people over the course of the next year. Mr. Stick's shell company makes arrangements to purchase a good portion of these "other" cars from the dealerships to make sure his company owns half the market. Each dealership still holds a large number of the 2011 models it must sell to make a profit and figures the cars it sold off to Mr. Stick were the same cars they would have to discount at the end of the model year anyway. The dealers are feeling pretty good about this figuring they can still sell the remaining cars for a nice profit and finish out the year ahead of the curve.

Now however, Mr. Stick begins playing his games. All of a sudden he puts all of the cars he has, half the entire inventory made, on the market. He dumps them for a small percentage of what he paid for them. He is willing to sell his entire inventory for $40 million. Despite the fact this is $10 million less than he paid for these cars; to this billionaire a lousy $10 million is a drop in the bucket.

The result however is; in order for the dealerships to compete, make any kind of profit and stay in business they must still sell their remaining cars for more money than they paid for them. This becomes very difficult because they must sell these cars for $5,500 while Mr. Stick is selling the same cars for $4,000!

The dealers can either dump the cars for $4,000 each or less and take a 20 percent loss on them or try to get the manufacturer to take them back. They may suggest the manufacturer offer some rebates to subsidize the dealers or sit on the cars trying to sell them hoping the market goes back up. By the time this happens though the 2012 models will come out. The dealerships which depend on Flood Cars for their new car sales are in a quandary. Some go out of business; others lay off employees or make other cutbacks. They complain loudly about what happened and the news media picks it up and chastises the Flood Cars Company which takes a major hit among stockholders.

Mr. Big Stick has done what he set out to do. All of his cars are gone, he only spent $10 million of his billions to achieve his goal and he has damaged the Flood Car Company. He is happy. For him it is no harm, no foul.

Where did he do this so quickly you ask? He did it on the Internet where sales are made in a hurry. He didn't set up a dealership and never paid a dime of rent. He had his own warehouses so housing the inventory was not a problem. All he had to do was ship the cars which cost him another million dollars.

Now this may seem like a farfetched scenario but considering high ticket items such as automobiles are the most difficult to use this theory, you get the picture about lesser priced businesses being targeted for something like this. The Internet is the main vehicle being used here because of its speed and its lack of controls.

Mr. Big Stick used predatory pricing on the Internet to destroy a reputable company and to damage if not put it out of business entirely along with many more small firms. It is a mess.

We brought the above scenario to a well known auto industry insider whom we trust. He obliged us on the condition his name not be used due to the sensitive nature of the inside industry discussion. He is an auto industry internet sales expert who works with sales reps at dealerships and teaches them about the new way of doing business. The Internet way. We asked him if the above scenario is a possibility. He didn't think it was at the moment but admits anything can happen in the changing Internet future. He sees other similarities however.

"In theory it could kind of work," he said. "I don't think it might happen now though."

Major changes have occurred because of price and because of the increasing use of the Internet. He calls it the Wal-Mart effect.

"If they need to, the larger dealerships can buy up and sell cars at ridiculously low prices almost like Wal-Mart and they drive the mom and pop dealerships out of business," he pointed out. "There are very few independent dealerships anymore; they are all large companies in the US."

And like a lot of businesses (see the baseball card industry) manufacturers play games based on allocations.

"Everybody in new cars deals with the manufacturer's rep and are allocated or sold a certain number of cars. They are often based on last year's sales and some other issues. They can't build an unlimited number of Camero's which is what happened in the past and caused problems. When they don't make enough cars then they start playing games. A dealer says look 'I need 25 Silverado 1500 Trucks' which are easy sellers and in short supply and high demand. The manufacturer says 'okay you have the 25 Silverados but you have to take 10 Luminas and 5 Geos to get them as part of the deal.'"

In other words take the two dogs and you'll get your hot selling vehicles. The dealership takes the dogs, makes his money on the trucks and dumps the Lumina and the Geo at cost or even below just to get rid of them. He runs a huge Internet ad which is less costly than newspaper and television and gets folks in with sweetheart deals. What does this do to the guy who maybe already has 10 or 15 of the Lumina and Geo cars and is slowly selling them for a nice profit? It means he either has to follow suit or get stuck with them and that means losing money.

"I honestly believe we will never technically lose the M-O we are operating under today, which is the way it's been as far back as I can remember," said our insider.

Lest you think him a dinosaur in believing in the lack of future change, he has already seen the change from the old business model to the new and they are light years apart.

"We call it a paradigm shift and your description of the way the Internet has changed the car business is, well you hit the nail on the head," he pointed out.

The expert explains, back in the 1980's and 1990's there were two ways to sell cars. First you had the walk-ins and then you had those who shopped from the newspaper advertisements. Newspaper ads were "price driven" and often involved a bait and switch technique. Putting hot low priced cars in the ads (of which there might be only one available) to draw the customer into the dealership. When the customer got there the car they saw in the ad had already been sold but there was a similar one with a much higher price tag.

"The car in the ad might not have had air, had roll up windows, vinyl compared to leather seats and possibly was a stick shift," he added. "Once they got to the dealership the salesman would offer them a similar car with upgrades for what turned out to be another $40 per month on their payment."

The Internet changed all of that for the most part.

"With the Internet people can obtain specific prices without leaving their home from a multitude of dealers which changes the way we do business on the phone and on the computer," he said. "The target is the same because the ultimate goal is to make an appointment and get the customer into the dealership, we actually don't want to close the deal on the phone, and we want to get you in to make the sale."

The insider explains if he's pushed by a customer on the phone or on-line to the point where the guy really is shopping price, he might eventually give in and give a price but doesn't want to. In most cases if a customer is a price shopper first and foremost he's not coming in until he gets the best price and he'll ignore the others. This often leads to frustration and there are times when some rough language can occur, usually from the customer.

"In being honest with the customer about a car I was offering I learned from the customer another salesman at another dealership he had spoken to had actually lied to him about the same car," he said. "The potential customer told me I was lying and he could get the car from the other company for two thousand dollars less and told me to go 'f—k myself'and I was the good guy telling the truth and I was the one getting screwed."

Our man doesn't see a major change in the way cars are sold due to the Internet in the near future because of what the product is.

"I think we are already there," he said. "We've found a new level if you will and this is how the business is going to be run."

The reason he points out is simple.

"They still want to come in to see it, smell it, drive it and that is the way the American public is used to buying cars, new cars," the instructor said. "In Europe it is not like this, they don't have large dealerships like we traditionally have."

Our expert went on to explain basically in Europe when you buy a car you go into an office, look through the brochures, pick out what you want and place the order. They don't keep huge inventories as American dealerships do where you have hundreds of cars to choose from. Land is much more valuable on the continent whereas in the United States you might have acres and acres of new cars from just one dealership.

Auto Malls were created for this purpose with an eye on the European style as well. Instead of thumbing through dozens of brochures you could come to one location and browse through a dozen different dealerships and a mile of new cars. The Internet has taken the Auto Mall to the next level.

"I don't see the European model coming to the United States although it may evolve down the road," he said. "The thing is timing; it takes a good 30 days to order a car with what you want. If you want something such as black leather it could take even more time depending on the workload at the factory. If you come into the dealership you drive out right now with your car."

So similar to the European Business Model, why don't manufacturers sell directly to the public on their own websites? Everyone else's industry does it but while our insider understands in the changing paradigm it could happen in his industry too, he says due to the different side angles of the business, it's not likely. Possible, and down the road who knows but right now it isn't likely.

"The missing piece of the puzzle is service, a huge part of what the dealership does is service the vehicles from warranties to general maintenance," he points out. "In theory the manufacturer could eliminate the dealership's service department by contracting with Joe's Automotive for service and to take care of warranties but the headaches would be huge. You still need the service industry which is over half of the pie and that is the key."

The logistics in the USA versus the logistics in say France or even Germany might be insurmountable as well.

"Can you imagine doing a national thing where the cars would either be shipped one by one from a central location or the customer had to drive three states away to pick up a vehicle?" He asked. "And the customer still can't touch it or feel it before they buy. You would need an avenue to deliver to the customer which right now the dealership provides."

There is precedent for direct sales to the customer through what is known as the Fleet Division. This is where a city, a county, a rental car company or a large business will buy their cars directly from the manufacturer but will get delivery through the local dealership. The entity may place an order for say 25 cars for its city employees to drive. An inexpensive deal is made directly with the manufacturer's Fleet Division and bypassing the local dealership. They still need a delivery system and that *is* the local dealership.

"The dealership may get a total of about $100 for participating in the program, and that is $100 total not per car," added our expert. "They basically provide a place for the manufacturer to park the cars until the customer can come and pick them up."

This all works of course because Americans at the moment are trusting corporate America. Everyone knows as the economy gets worse in certain times corporations look only at the bottom line and if the bottom line said to eliminate dealerships, they would. They did when General Motors and Chrysler moved toward bankruptcy and finally took billions of dollars in government bailouts in 2009-2010. Many dealerships had their contracts taken away basically putting some of them out of business as well as adding to the ranks of the unemployed.

"This really only affected a small number of people because let's be honest how many people *own* a car dealership?" He asked. "I honestly don't see much consolidation in the market due to the Internet or sales in general. Some are still struggling such as Chrysler, Jeep and Dodge, GM seems to be coming back and well Honda, Toyota and even Kia and Hyundai are on the upswing."

He still points to the individual American consumer as to why he believes despite changes there will always be a customer core to the automobile industry. It comes down to picking out a major purchase, much like buying a home.

"There are a certain number of grocery stores who offer Internet buying and if you have someone doing the buying for you and cooking your meals this works but for most people they have a thing about someone else picking out their produce or cuts of meat," said our expert. "What it comes down to is do you trust someone else to check the expiration date on the gallon of milk they are buying for you? If you buy cottage cheese you check the date but you can't be sure the person selecting it for you, from the store, will do the same."

He says it is the same with an automobile.

"Did they see the snag on the seat, was the rubber around the window fitting properly," he said. "We've had people have issues with the silliest things and we had to address this at the point of sale."

It might come down to a simple matter of did the seat feel right around your back and butt. The expert tells the story of the customer who was sold on a Hyundai because of the rear window shade. A 2006 Azera, a luxury model, has a window shade on the rear window to block the sun. This is operated by a button on the console. However, if the shade is up and the vehicle is put into reverse for backing up, the window shade automatically goes down so the driver can see. It goes back up when the car is put back into "Drive." The customer felt if the manufacturer had thought of this tiny little innovation they probably had thought of everything else as well.

"The customer was correct in his assumption, the manufacturer had probably taken care of the little details," said the salesman. "It all came down to taking care of the customer."

Overall, despite the changes in the business model due to the Internet and the job losses and the margins decrease, he feels the Internet has done one thing on the positive side.

"About 90-percent of the buyers we see use the Internet to get information which is not a bad thing," he said. "We like them to have information. The more information they have the easier they are to deal with because they won't go to more car dealers to make a decision. Some will, but really if you are the first guy on their list and you acknowledge them and make them the best deal you still have to allow them to do what they are going to do. If they have four on the list and they want to go to all four, you have to let them unless you can close the deal now."

This insider also acknowledges if he is the first guy on the list he has a good chance to close the deal before the customer goes to the other places. The customer obviously came to his first choice first, not his last. This is where the human touch takes over, a touch the Internet cannot provide. A good salesman who cares about the customer and the sale will usually close on the first try in a case such as this.

"It all comes back to the touchy feely thing," he added. "I do think the public is Internet savvy. They see a car on the road, on the freeway, in their neighborhood or at a show and they go right on-line to find out more so when they do end up coming to us they have a pretty good handle on what they want."

Armed with the information they need they start looking around. Maybe the Internet directs them to a certain dealership because it is close to their zip code. They start the communication and if the dealer is savvy as well they jump right on it. Not tomorrow, not next week, but right now and they start the conversation flowing. The idea is still to get them into the dealership where they can test drive the vehicle. The paradigm at this point is pretty much the same as in the old days but with a twist. Now the salesmen he trains are armed with something else. They know the customer is much more informed perhaps more than the salesman about the particular vehicle they want.

The salesmanship has changed. No longer is the hard sell the way to go. The customer has too much information to be snowballed or swayed, or switched.

"The American public still needs to see what they saw in the past though," he said. "You need to see the features and touch the car and those are the important factors to the sell. What motivates the buyer is they have to feel comfortable with the salesman."

He realizes sometimes it has to do with the manufacturer but not as much as in the past. Where your mom may have only purchased Chevrolets and your dad a Buick, today consumers are much more inclined to look at price first, what they want second and manufacturer third. It has become complicated with the many recalls over the last 20 years including the one which nearly devastated Toyota. Toyota by the way came out just fine in the end and still makes quality cars despite the bad press.

You still have the well heeled buyer who doesn't look at price first.

"You have your Costco Market and your Gelson's Market and you go to Gelson's knowing you are going to pay more but you go for the status, you can afford it," he details. "You go to Costco to save and maybe you even go to Food 4 Less where you have to bag your own groceries. It's the same way in the car business. If you are making $30,000 a month you pick out your top end car and write a check, but if you are the average guy making $50-$70 thousand a year you shop around a bit more and try to get the best price on what you have settled on. If you are in the $100,000 arena you are not as concerned with price."

In any case it is still a matter of getting them into the dealership and making the deal now. The bottom line is still the sale in American business.

"We are in business today and we know we can get the car they want in an hour by trading it with another dealership if we have to, that would be ideal but we don't want to get into a 30 day buying cycle. We don't want them thinking things over, the coffee gets clouded and they see an ad on the Super Bowl and say 'wow I didn't know Chevy made that or Ford made that.' If that happens we're into a whole new ballgame."

So why won't the European model work? It obviously does there and would lend itself more directly to Internet sales from the manufacturer to the consumer.

"The Internet was a huge game changer because it stopped our walk-in traffic per se and they channeled their way first through the Internet," answered our point man. "It made all the dealerships get better on the Internet and on the phones and I train people to deal with this new MO."

The bottom line still is the American car buyer, while grasping the Internet as part of the package, still has to come in and feel and touch and select. He doesn't want to buy from a brochure. Buying a new car to Americans isn't like buying out of the Sears Catalog. This may change but this expert doesn't feel it will change soon. The key to selling cars today is the public and its fears.

"The American public has a fear of commitment and they use the Internet to express this," he said. "They will say things in an email from a keyboard they would never tell you in person to your face. This has made the job much harder."

Let us take a different kind of business with a little lower price tag. You don't have to create a better mousetrap to do this. All you have to do is control the market the mousetrap is in. Some of it is through legitimate competition.

Blockbuster takes a huge hit because Netflix stole its market but it stole it in a legitimate way. Americans no longer purchased VHS, DVD or even rented them by going to the Blockbuster store to pick them up and bring them back. Netflix made it so the consumer could download the same movie while sitting on their sofa at home and they could get it on demand.

Blockbuster began discounting prices several years ago. At one time it was $5 to rent a video. If you didn't bring it back the next day there was a late fee which could amount to anywhere from a dollar to the rental cost of the video depending on how long you kept it. That didn't work too well so they dropped the late fees for certain things.

When Netflix arrived on the scene they were offering the same basic service for the same price via return mail. You could keep the DVD for a week or more and return it to get another with no late fee.

Then along came the Internet, HD, DVD and home versions of everything under the sun. Soon, for $.99 Netflix was offering consumers the right to download the video they wanted to see directly to their home computer or television box. Blockbuster was dead. First it could not compete on price or delivery system especially since Netflix moved into the next step; how about several weeks of downloaded videos for $9.99 or even less with special deals?

How could Netflix charge so little and still stay in business? It costs virtually nothing to download a movie. So making a few cents per download millions of times a week adds up to some pretty big dollars. When you don't have the overhead, you don't have the staff and you have the customers who are willing to pay so little for so much, you are going to be successful.

Was this predatory pricing? Not really because what Netflix did was invent a better mousetrap. They didn't beat Blockbuster at its own game, they invented a new game. The new game was the download. The Internet is full of downloads.

Remember the porn industry we talked about?

In 1955 you could purchase what was called a "blue" movie on reel to reel, 16 millimeter movie film. If you could find one of these bootleg reels it usually involved anywhere from one to several people performing sex acts in silence. Occasionally you might find one with sound.

As laws changed and society got more liberal "live" theatres opened up and replaced the now gone Burlesque Theatres of the 1940's and 1950's. These live theatres offered live sex acts on stage. They still faced local ordinances but the larger cities still had them until someone invented Video Tape for home use. The VHS and BETA home players and recorders were all the rage.

Soon these theatres were offering any adult the chance to see new porno films at places such as The Pussy Cat Theatre to name just one. Where you might have gone to see a live sex act for $20 you could now go to see one on the big screen for $5. When DVD's came out VHS was gone and with the advent of home VHS, the theatres were gone as well. With the loss of those theaters went another 10 to 20 jobs, more or less. These were ticket sellers, concessionaires, doormen, ushers and office workers.

Why pay $5 or even less to sit in a dingy old movie house smelling of cheap booze and perverts when you could watch such films from the privacy of your own bedroom with your spouse or bed mate? You also didn't have to check the street before you went in to make sure none of your friends were watching you enter the seedy movie house.

Enter the Internet where porn began to boom. At first it cost money just like any of the theatres which preceded it. However this business model seemed to fit the Internet perfectly. At first there were charges for downloading porn videos. Soon however there were free sites going up everywhere. Doing a search on the Internet for "free porn clips" you can find thousands of short sex sessions which are free and entirely safe.

Most people who want Internet porn don't want the dangers of A) someone finding out about it such as their wife or husband, and B) the chance to get a computer virus. Both evidently are real dangers in this modern world of safe sex.

So how does one make money by giving pornography away on the internet? It is not that hard when you consider the reasons for giving it away. The more the customer gets for free the more he comes back. Eventually he/she want more and with a simple click and a credit card they can "subscribe" to something more on a regular basis rather than a two minute sex act for a teaser.

Of course, and here comes the dangerous part, they can get caught in the Continuity Game which we described in the previous chapter. They have your credit card and they keep charging it for a small fee, say $5 per month, every month until you call and cancel. That is if you remember to do so and this is never a guarantee.

It is not predatory pricing, it is not illegal and while it does say "Buyer Beware" all over it, it happens all the time on the Internet. When someone tells you Porn is the biggest thing on-line they are pretty much correct. Porn is busting out all over and the really sad thing about it is, it's very easy to get content.

There is another factor involved here. Advertising. If you give something away on the Internet you get lots of "hits" to your site. By getting more hits you get more people on your site and if you survey them as to their age, gender and spending habits you have something to provide to advertisers. These are advertisers who see you are getting 100,000 unique users each day and they want to be seen by those people. They now want to advertise on your site.

You now have someone to pay for that little bit of cash you shell out each month to run your site. Advertising is the key and getting people to use your site by giving away its content will bring advertisers into the fold.

Business Terrorism on the Internet

You have already seen how one person can, with a plan and not so much money, destroy a legitimate business by playing games through e-commerce on the Internet. You have also seen how someone with lots of money, billions or more can destroy other businesses on the Internet in the same way. More money, more power. This is nothing new in American or even world economics. Money powers the game and the game is greed.

However, what if an international terrorist group wanted to destroy an American business? Or many American businesses? Or, Capitalism itself? Could it be done?

Why not? Of course it could be done.

So far terrorists led by the late Osama Bin Laden chose to destroy the American way of life through terror via blood. The 9-11 terrorist attack was first of all an attack on American Capitalism. The means through which Al Qaeda chose to destroy the Twin Towers in New York was utterly stupid. You don't bring down a country by frightening its people. If you do this you only create more of a resolve to fight against you.

No the way you bring down a country in the modern world is through its economy. The attack on 9-11 was at the heart of the American economy it was believed. They struck the World Trade Center believing this was the heart of our economic way of life. It wasn't Wall Street but it did have lots of stock traders. It did not work. The following war in Afghanistan didn't even hurt the US economy. It was the war in Iraq combined with other factors which complicated matters and helped drive the current economy into near ruin.

The way again to destroy a country is by bringing down its economy and not by killing people. If Osama Bin Laden had been smarter he would have used his billions from his royal family and directed them at destroying American businesses in the manner described above. He wouldn't even have had to break any laws to do it. He could have used smart people from all over the world on the Internet to destroy business by business after business and bring the US economy to its knees.

What kind of businesses could he have targeted? First he would not want to target the housing and mortgage industries. Those are already so screwed up why bother. Besides the cost of doing business would be too much.

Such a terrorist should start small and get established. A recent edition of the CBS Show "60 Minutes" pointed out how being an Internet company close to Wall Street can make all the difference in destroying a business.

On May 6, 2010, the Dow Industrials plunged 600 points in a matter of just a few minutes sending shockwaves through the financial system, Washington and the country in general. The market recovered those 600 points in almost the same amount of time. Consumer confidence in the market was shaken for a long time afterward. What happened?

Computers now perform well over half the trading on Wall Street today. In some cases they are set up as super computers by companies who have no interest in the market except to make money. The computers are programmed using mathematical formulas with one intention; see a trend coming and buy the stock before it goes up. The next move would be to sell it off just as quickly to turn a profit.

Millions of trades are made like this each day by these computers. On May 6 what triggered the 20 minute market collapse was a mutual fund computer dumped $4.1 billion of securities in those 20 minutes. Those securities were grabbed quickly by the super computers and sold almost immediately. This action triggered other computers and soon the market had what was called a mini-crash. Fortunately the system was reversed and the market regained those shares. However, the damage had been done. Within months investors pulled $70 billion out of the market because they were scared for the most part. They did not trust the system.

This was an unexpected phenomenon and since that time some control triggers were placed on the system. This doesn't mean the system can not be hit again. Given a computer and knowledge someone else at some point will find a way to crack the system. We can only hope it is not a terrorist who does it and then uses this knowledge to carry out a daring attack.

Destroying a business which sells hard goods as well as consumable goods would be the most likely target. Food industries would be easy to do, entertainment industries would not. The music industry has already shot itself in the foot with the download story. It didn't take much to make it so artists can't make a living at what they do whether they are musicians or actors or singers.

No it would have to be hard goods or nothing. Parts for key things Americans consume would be a nice target, any kind of staples which are in shorter supply and rather on the expensive side would be better. Finding the right business to destroy is a key and then following on the success of this destruction and learning from the mistakes would lead to more destruction. Attacking a city's water supply, electrical grid, gas lines or even traffic systems could cause havoc for any community. Eventually a major dent would be made in the economy.

In September, 2011, California found out the hard way how vulnerable utilities are. One lone worker in Arizona pushed the wrong switch basically and put five million Americans in the dark for hours. Nearly all of the Coachella Valley south of Palm Springs was blacked out sending people scrambling for supplies at local stores. It also shut out the lights in parts of Arizona and New Mexico. It even shut down some power south of the border in Northern Mexico.

Federal investigators met with officials at North American Electric Reliability Corporation to determine what happened. The first thought was a terrorist attack. It wasn't. The following day

California Governor Jerry Brown pointed out how fragile the state's infrastructure really was calling it "brittle."

"Brittle power means its easy to break," the governor told KNX 1070 News Radio in a phone interview. "We're in a brave new world here and we're going to have to make the investments and the regulatory efforts."

The problem is these terrorists like to make a statement and just tearing down society isn't enough. They will keep trying to blow up airplanes and cause havoc and in the end they will fail because people resist such acts. Taking the soft approach, behind the scenes makes sense but terrorism in all its forms doesn't make sense. It is hoped the Osama's of the world will leave the economy alone but terrorists are not exactly the greatest minds in the world and reason often doesn't come into play.

CBS Anti-terrorism expert Professor Raymond Tanter says one major attempt at economic terrorism was averted when a UPS plane was leaving Saudi Arabia and an act of attempted terrorism was averted in September 2010. Two packages of explosives were found on board which were to be delivered to synagogues in Chicago.

"The world is a closed village with respect to technology and Fed Ex, UPS and the United States Postal Service work with computerized systems which terrorists can take advantage of," he said. "If those planes had gone down ecommerce would have come to a halt and your book would have been passé."

He believes while terrorism in the sky remains a major threat, the sea lanes will be the next major terrorist target to disrupt commerce.

"The next frontier of vulnerability will be the sea cargo areas such as the ports of Long Beach, Baltimore and Houston where millions of goods are shipped to in a much less expensive venture than by air," Tanter stated. "The air cargo system will be tightened up and the vulnerabilities will exist at sea."

Of course Somali pirates have been taking this route for a decade now by reaching out and snatching cargo ships. Usually they are held for ransom along with the crews, with the pirate war lords getting rich in the process sitting in lawless Somalia. Tanter believes the threat of Al Qaeda is still in existence but more from the branch networks rather than the central command.

"Al Qaeda of the Arabian Peninsula is manned by American born terrorists who handled the Ft. Hood massacre and the Nigerian who was the-would-be Times Square bomber," he said. "So I suspect as Al Qaeda central decreases, the affiliates will emerge as number one and this is where the group on the Arabian Peninsula is internet savvy."

You only have to point to the Arab Spring which used the Internet (specifically Face Book and Twitter) to help topple governments in Tunisia, Egypt and Libya and caused havoc in Yemen and Syria among others.

Name Your Price

Priceline.com is the prime example of what works well on the Internet followed by eBay and every other auction site on the World Wide Web. The idea of increasing margins to make more money has gone away with the Internet. It's been replaced by the Buy It Now or Name Your Price way of doing business. In other words let the consumer pay what they want, not what the business wants or needs to sell it for.

This entire thought process would have the founding fathers scratching their heads. They were businessmen first and foremost. Some would say they were businessmen before they were patriots. Look how long it took them to remove the blight of slavery from the land. Slavery was good for business.

The real model for a successful business is to sell your goods or services for a reasonable profit. That profit is then used, as stated earlier, to make the owner a living, expand the business and increase employment opportunities. In time a 30 percent profit margin for goods would be increased to 35 percent and perhaps 40 percent as the business grew. With competition the profit margin might shrink but the idea was to make the business so strong consumers would want the product at whatever the price. The best part of that idea was to make a product and build the firm's reputation so competition would either work harder or go away. This was what was behind a growing and successful business.

The Internet has brought a halt to this and started a new trend. The new trend is to give it to the consumer at the lowest possible price and hopefully they will return out of loyalty. A consumer who buys from a business because the firm had the lowest price is not going to return out of loyalty. Next time they need the product that certain business sells they will once more search for the best price. If they find it cheaper somewhere else they will buy it somewhere else. Loyalty is not gained by having the best price. Loyalty is gained by offering the best products and best service. Price should be an afterthought.

Priceline is a prime example of the way not to do business when it comes to repeat business and loyalty. Priceline soon found the competition great and it was forced to start offering different ways of doing business because it could not compete.

Under the original theory consumers would name their price. However, if Priceline gave them a room or an airline flight at that price they had to take it. They were charged for it if Priceline found one at the price requested.

Here is an example. For my daughter's 21st birthday three of us were going to Las Vegas. We didn't have a lot of money at the time and we were only going on an overnight outing so an inexpensive hotel room was desired. After checking the hotels themselves booking a room for three people for one night at the lowest available price of $189.00 was out of the question. We decided to try Priceline.

I started by putting in a ridiculously low $25 as the most I would pay. Priceline requires you put your credit card number into the search. If they have the room you are locked in and your card will be charged. Not surprisingly there were no rooms for $25. We bumped it up to $50 figuring again there would be no rooms available. Much to my surprise there was a Ramada Inn Express Suites for up to four people for $50. My card was immediately charged and we had our room. This was great. The only question was in what kind of neighborhood and shape was this hotel?

We were very pleased with the hotel and happy with the service. While small it was clean, had two bedrooms, free breakfast, pool and all the amenities. We only needed the place for one night and it had three beds along with fresh coffee and tea in the room. We were happy and the trip went well.

The next time we were in a similar situation was a trip to Sacramento. Again we thought we'd go through Priceline. The cheapest hotel was $65. Since Priceline did not offer a "look around" the neighborhood or an address or photo of the place, we went blind.

Upon arriving at the hotel the hookers hanging around on the corner meant Priceline kept the money on the card and we drove on to another hotel farther down the road. Priceline was now "off" our list of services to use for hotels.

Soon other on-line Travel Agents were offering the same deals but with more consumer friendly options. You could at least see the rooms on video, the neighborhoods and in some cases but not all, you could even call the hotel to find out the agency, not the hotel had the best price.

Travelocity, Cheap Tickets, Orbitz and many others were springing up all over. They were offering the same basic service Priceline was offering but with better consumer options. Soon Priceline was forced to do the same. While keeping their core service of Name Your Own Price with minor changes, they offered an upgrade service similar to the other travel agents for an additional fee. They had become just like Orbitz, Travelocity and the rest but their core service still set them apart. It wasn't far apart but those who were searching for "price only" still had that option.

In the long run all of these services soon began offering rooms and rates and air fares at basically the same price. They learned you can only give stuff away for free for so long before you go out of business and many of these companies did exactly that. Being the cheapest in order to gain new customers means you eventually have to sell at break even or at a loss. Both mean you will be out of business very quickly.

eBay used its patented "Buy It Now" as an alternative to auctions which run from three to 10 days. The eBay auction site was so successful the company CEO Meg Whitman retired with billions of dollars and made a run at the governorship of the state of California. She spent her own money in what became the most expensive campaign in state history and one of the costliest in the history of the country. She lost, by the way, to former Governor Jerry Brown, a frugal man always who spent a small percentage of what Whitman shelled out.

When eBay engineered its auction program it was designed to be the world's swap meet or garage sale. It worked well. Soon people were using the site to run an auction business. They even began going to real garage sales to buy stuff to sell on eBay. These folks began developing their own business models before eBay began changing rapidly.

Upon seeing this phenomena eBay executives decided to cater to this market. Once the thrill of eBay wore off and with new but not so serious competition looming, they chose to offer sellers the opportunity to own an "eBay Store." This was an actual on-line or virtual store where people could go to shop on-line and buy things at a fixed price. Executives were pushing harder and harder to get people to list things in these stores by dropping the "listing price." Where a typical seven day auction for an item which sold for $100 would net eBay about $3 for doing absolutely nothing but being the facilitator, eBay soon offered 30-day fixed price in-store sales much cheaper. This was an effort to get more listings albeit at a lower price.

eBay charged $.30 to list an item for seven days and then took a small commission. There were extra fees for extra services such as **"bold print"** in your listing or adding extra photographs. There was also a commission once the sale ended. For the 30-day store listing eBay decided to charge only $.03 for the listing plus commission.

Thousands of sellers opened these stores encouraged by the low price. Why list 100 items at $.30 four times in a month when you could list the same 100 items for $.03 for the entire month. The former would cost $120 while the latter was only $3! It was a no brainer, especially if you were selling items which did not move very rapidly.

So the new eBay plan to get more listings at cheaper prices eventually backfired. Within a couple of years executives decided it wasn't making as much money as the old way and started encouraging people to put more stuff up for auction rather than in eBay stores. When sellers didn't rush to join the newest program officials chose to offer incentives such as listing their items higher in the "search engine" if the item was up for "auction" rather than "in-store." They started tinkering with the pricing structure to get more people to take their items from the stores and put them up for auction.

One of the strangest moves came in mid-2010. Since many of the items in the stores were duplicates eBay forced the issue. The company automatically removed a seller's duplicate item.

For instance, if a seller was selling four copies of the same book in their eBay store for $4.00, eBay automatically removed three of them. They would not do this if the four books were auctioned off separately in a limited time auction.

Another move by eBay forced the key issue at hand. Many sellers tried to up the profit margin by charging "shipping & handling." This has been a common practice since the inception of the United States Postal Service. You might sell an item for a very little margin but try to make up some of it in the S&H costs. If an item cost you $4 and you sold it for $5 you might charge $3 for shipping and handling even though it only cost $1 to ship it. Pocketing the other $2 is a legitimate expense when you figure in packaging materials and the time in packing and taking it to the Post Office to ship. A $2 charge for this is not out of the question. Some people would even charge more and often that might not be enough.

The good folks at eBay decided this should not happen. After all, why should sellers actually make a few dollars on their items? The company put a maximum of $4 on shipping books citing the lower cost of "Media Mail," to ship books. They started giving demerits for people they felt were charging too much for shipping and even in their rating system for feedback it is weighted toward the cost and service of shipping.

Then they decided sellers could not leave feedback for buyers. Buyers however were encouraged to leave feedback for sellers. The feedback system was another unique idea from eBay. When a transaction was made both the seller and the buyer were originally encouraged to give a Yes or a No to the results of the transaction. If everything went well and the items and the payments were good then you would leave a Positive Feedback. If something was amiss you could either leave a Neutral or a Negative which basically had the same effect.

After the year 2000 however eBay changed the policy. It felt sellers were unfairly leaving "retaliatory feedback" by leaving negatives when they were not warranted. So while a seller could "respond" to negative feedback from a buyer, the seller could not "leave" negative feedback for the buyer. Evidently eBay officials in their infinite wisdom decided Buyers were incapable of leaving retaliatory feedback. Many sellers decided this was a joke and chose never to leave feedback unless requested since it was now useless information and a meaningless waste of time.

The Media Mail for books was also somewhat of a joke. A heavy book sent across the country, such as an art book was still expensive with media mail. For instance, in October 2010 my company shipped an art book within the state of California using Media Mail. We charged the customer $7 for the book and the eBay limit of $4 for shipping. The shipping charge was actually $5.35. The postal clerk, whose wife is an eBay seller, asked if he could check the price if it were going to New York. I said okay. The Media Mail price for this book to New York? It was $36! eBay did make changes in the book shipping arena.

On the positive side, eBay does allow book sellers to charge whatever they want to ship internationally. We took a real hit on one of these. An art book we sold on-line went for $7 but we did cover ourselves with a $20 shipping charge. There is no Media Mail for overseas so you have to ship first class. It was $26.89.

We also paid $2.29 for a shipping envelope and of course eBay took their fees. I paid a man in Paris basically to take the book off my hands! That was not predatory pricing but what it was turned out to be a lack of research on our part. It obviously wasn't planned that way.

eBay kept its Buy It Now program but all it has done is to make more people lazy sellers on the Internet and put more stuff into eBay's data base. It does not provide a good research tool since many people who offer a Buy It Now price are overpricing the item and they often sit for months or even years without selling. They are trying to get a good, if not outrageous profit margin as in a store front. Listing such an item on eBay is counterproductive certainly and usually a waste of time.

Ask any regular eBay seller how many items he's had in his eBay store for years and they have not sold and you will get a raised eyebrow with the answer "too many." The reason is these are people who understand a profit margin based business model. They may understand the Internet business model as well. They just don't like it and can't adhere to it.

Fewer young sellers/consumers understand the idea of "not losing money" as compared to older sellers. Most older people I've spoken with in my dealings as a representative for a major auction house (Huggins & Scott Auctions) often tell me they just want to get back what they paid for the item. In other words they want to sell their items but they don't want to lose money doing it. Unfortunately the Internet has become quite a bit about losing money, or taking what you can get for it.

One older man, likely about 75 years old and a former banking executive, called me and wanted to sell his stuff but didn't want to auction it. He was willing to take much less than what he felt it was worth if he could be assured of cash in hand rather than taking a chance on the Internet for auctions. He also wanted to sell it all and not break it up.

I made the trip to find over 900 square feet of memorabilia in a very nice neighborhood. There were lots of vintage items and some very rare ones. Without doing an inventory I could not get an accurate count and since he wasn't willing to auction it this really didn't matter anyway. My job now was to find him a buyer.

"I really think there is $500,000 worth of stuff here, retail price, and I should be asking about $220,000," the man told me. "I all together have spent $150,000 on this stuff so that is all I want to get out of it."

We discussed the possibilities and the fact since the inception of the Internet, whether you sold it there or not, there really was no retail and wholesale anymore. It was all the same because the line had been obliterated. He understood which is why he felt $150,000 was fair and he was not going to sell it for less than he paid for it.

I understood and we worked out a commission basis for me if I did indeed bring him a successful buyer. The bottom line though here is he understood, as a businessman, you can't sell for less than what you paid. Try telling this to a 20-something who has grown up on the Internet and only wants to "get a deal."

These new consumers don't usually understand there is a price for doing business. If you sell something it had to cost you something, somewhere. Unless it was a gift you have something into it, some money. To buy it for $99 and turn around and sell it for $90 means you lost $9. There is no other way to put it. And if you keep buying it for $99 and selling it for $90 you soon won't have any money to buy any more. Putting this type of seller out of business is probably a good thing.

Even the Internet model for business of just making enough to get something positive is a losing situation. Buying for $99 and selling for $100 is not a profit. As we noted in the chapter about Baseball Cards 101 it is a losing proposition and has only been put into motion in a much faster and more common way with the Internet.

As we have seen by the above examples "Name Your Price" just doesn't work. Consumers are fickle. Yes, they shop price and in today's world they usually shop price first. This is unless they are the well heeled and smart consumer. The higher end so to speak. This is where traditionally business is always good and price is not the object of first desire.

Take any business in the world. The smart money always goes with the "higher end" or the "luxury class." There is a company in the San Francisco Bay area which only deals with the higher end of the travel world. Travel Wizard in San Raphael,

California near San Francisco is one of those luxury travel agencies dealing mainly on the web. Bob McMillen set out to service the best and isn't interested in being inexpensive. He has one of the top luxury travel agencies in the world. Even their email concierge.com speaks volumes about high end service and clientele.

The company set its sites high, ventured with Virtuoso which is a conglomerate of high end luxury travel agents, and services former White House staffers and key personnel. McMillen told me when we were discussing some business options several years ago, he offers a lower end service but only if someone calls and insists upon it. His company is only interested if you are going to spend big bucks, you want the luxurious end of travel and you are not interested in Europe on $100 day.

The end result is his company is very successful and will continue to be successful as long as they put out the service and as long as they charge whatever they have to in making their clients feel special, pampered and as if they actually have the money they are spending. Do they overcharge? They charge what their customers are willing to pay and like so many other companies in the same boat so to speak, they charge a lot. Priceline customers need not apply. They are not rude. If you can afford them they will treat you very well and if not they will turn you over to someone else.

What we commonly call the high end usually doesn't shop on the Internet first although they are making inroads now they have the access. Usually there is a buffer between them and the actual purchasing. There is someone they employ to do the purchasing but they themselves are going on line more often than in previous years.

Who buys million dollar pieces of art? Someone who can afford to hire someone to find the million dollar pieces of art. Who buys luxury homes? Someone with a Beverly Hills real estate agent. The sellers today however are marketing their wares on the Internet but when it comes to the higher end products they still work off client lists and contacts. The lookilu's are searching the Internet in most cases when it comes to luxury items. Those who buy them on the Internet usually find themselves purchasing a knockoff from Baidu or some other Chinese web site.

High end sellers, whether it is antiques, art, baseball cards or homes, unless it is at auction, don't shop on the Internet. Sellers of such goods may offer them on the Internet but those who are buying are in the vast majority of cases "contacts," not Internet surfers.

The bottom line is when it comes to the high end it is business as usual and business remains good despite recessions, economic downturns and Bull Markets. In the non-virtual world of business its quality first, service second and price last. On the Internet it's price first, price second and price third. Quality, like an infomercial, is far down the list.

A successful long term businessperson deals in the high end. There is more money to be made, there is a much higher profit margin and the contacts and buyers (with certain exceptions) are less likely to quibble over price. If you want to run a small business you can still run it dealing with the higher end. The cost of doing business and the barrier to entry is much higher. Success and the number of headaches however are going to be quite different than if you run a small business from home selling items on the Internet making margins of 1 to 2 percent. You may make more sales but will make a lot less money than if you make a few sales to the higher end.

You won't even have to worry about the price. Selling to the luxury class means selling it for more than you ever thought you would get for it. You start high and you end high. Remember, price is not the key in dealing with the luxury market. If they want it they will pay for it and they have enough money to do that, so take it and move on.

They won't be surfing the web for a better price. You can bet on it.

The Founding Fathers

Ever wonder what the Founding Fathers would have thought about the Internet? Certainly they never could have imagined it, which has given the Supreme Court fits in recent years. There is not much laid out in the Constitution about cyberspace and the virtual world. One thing for certain though is they would not have liked the word "e-commerce" in the way it is practiced today.

In a word the Founding Fathers were "businessmen" first and foremost. John Adams and Thomas Jefferson were both farmers who in Jefferson's case used slaves to run his plantation. So did George Washington. Adams ran a much smaller family farm and farmed out his kids so to speak to work it along with wife Abigail.

Benjamin Franklin was a publisher and the Good Lord knows what else. He had his hands in any number of businesses including the First United States Post Office. When he wasn't wooing the ladies at the Court of France he was making money in a whole lot of enterprises.

Paul Revere, Patriot and night rider to sound the alarm was a Silversmith who ran a small business in Boston. Of the 55 signers of the Declaration of Independence 25 were lawyers, 13 were merchants, six were land speculators, 11 were speculators in securities, a dozen owned or managed slaves on plantations and large farms, two owned small farms, eight were career politicians, three were retired businessmen, two were scientists, two were doctors and one was a college president. A few were wealthy but most were average working people doing a variety of jobs.

In other words they were working men who understood business, profit and buying and selling. Whether they were selling corn on the open market or putting a case before a judge they were businessmen first. A lot of folks would have you believe they were something else. Yes they were patriots and great men, but they were businessmen who saw their livelihoods being ripped apart by a foreign king and this was making business bad.

Think of it this way. King George III was the Internet and Tom Jefferson and Benny Franklin and the boys realized making a six pence profit was not going to keep them in business. They needed to make Pounds and if they couldn't make Pounds they might as well make Dollars under their own flag.

The United States wasn't founded on the freedom of Religion; it wasn't founded on the principle of one man-one vote. It was founded on the simple premise the colonists screamed out loud in their rebellion leading up to the war of the revolution; "No taxation without representation!" There was the Boston Tea Party where patriots tossed British Tea into the harbor over taxes. The Stamp Act was another way to tax the colonials. When it came right down to it, it was all about MONEY. Money, Money, Money and more Money. The colonials hit the British where it hurt most; in the pocketbook.

It wasn't freedom of speech, religion, race, creed or color. The only color which really mattered was what we now call "green" which is the color of the All American Dollar. If it was about religion why were Jews and Catholics persecuted in the South? If it was about race why where the Chinese persecuted and discriminated against and if it were about color why was slavery allowed to exist? Why was the American Indian or Native American moved off his good land to awful land?

Jews and Catholics held a large portion of the money in the United States. There again is that money issue. The Chinese were cheap labor to build the railroads. Black slaves were the cheapest labor of all. The American Indian lived in places where the land was good; gold was plentiful as were buffalo and elk. Does any of this smack of money?

The Founding Fathers set the tone from the beginning. Money was the key as it always is. Don't get me wrong, the American public was in the same boat. They all wanted to work, to be free to conduct their business and to make as much money as they could for their family and make a good life in general. These are inalienable rights certainly and there is nothing wrong with any of this. Just realize it for what it is; money is at the heart of it all. Power and money and what is power but putting money to a stronger and more persuasive use.

So let us place the Founding Fathers and their constituents into the 21st Century and the age of the Internet. Where would they have gone with it?

Bedford, Blair, Clymer, Dayton, Fitzsimons, Franklin, King, Langdon, Robert Morris, Charles Cotesworth, Pinckney and

Sherman were all financial speculators on a large scale. Wall Street would be their home basically. Would they have fallen victim to the rigors and pressures of today's Wall Street, the Wall Street of Gordon Gekko's "Greed is Good?" Some would have certainly. Human nature being what it is, they would have been tempted.

The fast workings of Internet stock trading caused real problems in the financial markets and to excuse any of the above men from possibly falling into that trap would be inexcusable. There would have been problems.

Blount, Dayton, Fitzsimons, Gorham, Robert Morris and Wilson were land speculators. The housing market would be their place today. A couple would be weathering out the storm, a couple would be broke most likely having used their homes like an ATM (something else they would have deplored) and a couple might have seen the stupidity of "Sub Prime Lending" and waited out the storm to purchase dozens of expensive homes at cheap prices on speculation.

The three retired gentlemen would really be worried today. Franklin would be okay as he had his hands in so many things. McHenry and Mifflin might just have seen their 401K go down the drain and trying desperately to get back involved to get some income. Hopefully they didn't have a reverse mortgage backfire on them.

Williamson the scientist would be in for a really rough time. With the government squeeze on in a big way grants for scientific projects are drying up. Unless he invented an electric car getting 5000 miles to the charge, he'd be sunk. Whoops, Franklin already invented that one. Don't worry about Benjy, he's doing okay in any universe.

Dr. McClurg is complaining about the lack of Medicare payments. He isn't taking any new patients but he's still doing well with the ones he has. He did lay off some office staff.

The 13 we should be most worried about are those who were merchants at the time of the Convention and who didn't have other things to fall back on. Of the 13 who solely had to rely on their merchant status there were a few who had little else to show for their hard work. Shields, Gilman and Pierce would be the guys most affected by the Internet. They were merchants with wares to sell and unless they adapted very quickly they would be sunk. It doesn't matter what they dealt in because over the centuries goods change. Lawyers don't but goods do. Of course in Pierce's case it probably wouldn't have mattered anyway. He did suffer a series of financial reverses and ended up in bankruptcy. He might have done well with the Internet.

If for instance they normally bought their goods for say $20 per item from a distributor and sold them for $40 per item to their customers, it would soon be over. Those same $20 items sold to them to re-sell to their customers are now being sold by the manufacturer for $22 directly to the public. This now means Shields, Gilman and Pierce would have to sell the items to their customers who remained for either $22 to compete or take a chance on loyal customers who might pay $24.

Since we have already shown above there is no loyalty on the Internet because price is first on-line, Shields, Gilman and Pierce would probably get few takers. There you have it. The Internet has just run three of the Founding Fathers out of business. Wow.

Now this game of speculation above is all well and good but the reality is if the Internet had been around in 1776 the Founding Fathers might have found a way to make it so there was "some" barrier to entry. They would have realized the stupidity of a society which has to make a profit to survive and attempted to kill those profits in the name of ease of use. In many cases it is exactly that; ease of use rather than just plain ordinary efficiency.

Franklin, Washington, Adams and even the more liberal ideas of Jefferson would have understood nothing comes for free which is worth getting. Jefferson realized this when he freed his slaves shortly after the founding of the country. If it is worth doing it is worth paying for. Yes price matters to the vast majority of people. It doesn't matter to the Luxury crowd we discussed in the last chapter. It matters to some degree to everyone else.

The counterpoint is the worst part of the equation. By buying via price only on the Internet you inadvertently destroy legitimate business and real jobs.

In her campaign for Governor of California former eBay CEO Meg Whitman touted her creation of thousands of jobs at eBay and creating thousands of new businesses and businesspeople around the world. Yes jobs were created at eBay as the company expanded. The "new" jobs she created for businesspeople around the world were people thinking they were going into business for themselves by creating eBay stores. At best these were commission based, no-benefits jobs created on the backs of people who thought they had a future by working for themselves. At worst they were hopes and promises chugging along at the will of eBay and its stockholders looking to improve the bottom line. As those "new businesses" began to fall away the stockholders got discouraged, eBay raised fees and changed rules and Whitman left a billion dollars richer.

These were not new jobs created by eBay. It was eBay destroying thousands of small mom and pop businesses and even larger companies around the world. It meant the laying off of 40 hour a week workers who were no longer needed because manufacturers were now selling directly to consumers on the Internet via eBay and their own websites. They were mid level employees who did sales, and other long time jobs. Shipping departments grew and the US Postal Service teamed with eBay to cater to the giant auction site on packaging ideas. Jobs created? Jobs lost.

There is no way to tell for sure but it is very likely the Internet has cost more jobs than it's created counting home businesses which came about. Many of those home businesses were started because people lost their legitimate jobs, with benefits and seniority, due to the Internet and led by the surge of eBay.

The public continues to perpetuate the myth of buying cheaper is necessary. Homemaker A says she is always looking for a bargain so she shops on-line. She is looking for a winter coat for her daughter. Sears has the coat she wants and the price is $69. She gets all the information off the coat and begins an on-line search. She finds it at Sears On-Line store and website. Sears is selling the same coat it has in the store for the lower price of $59 with free shipping. She is flabbergasted. If Sears can sell her the coat for $59 on line and free shipping, why can't they sell it to her in the store for $59 instead of $10 more?

She is upset at Sears and she continues searching on-line. She finds the same coat at some discount web seller for $29 plus $5 Shipping. She can get the same coat for $34 or about half the price she can get it from the main store which is selling it in her neighborhood. She clicks away and buys the $34 coat.

Two weeks later she is talking to her friend at lunch who works at Sears.

"I just got laid off from Sears," her friend says.

"Why what happened?" Asks Shopper A.

"Business is slow, so many people are shopping on-line we had a 25 percent staff reduction across the board at the local store and more to come at the other chain stores," is her reply. "No one is coming into the store when they can just buy from the convenience of home and for less money."

Shopper A is too embarrassed to tell her friend about the coat. She realizes she has contributed to the loss of her friend's job in a small way. By shopping by price only she has helped take a job away from a friend. Will she continue to shop on-line for price? Probably. It is the same reason she continued to shop at Wal-Mart over the years.

Price shopping kills jobs, it does not create them. The Internet is the greatest killer of jobs in the world today and while it does create new ones the new jobs are not usually enough to pay the bills and live comfortably in today's world. It is only going to get worse as long as there is no barrier to entry.

The Clinton Initiative and Job Growth

While his vice-president Al Gore lays claim to inventing the Internet, President Bill Clinton says they knew before the World Wide Web became a reality, it would destroy the business model. It had to. In a 2011 interview with Yahoo, the former President explained during what was being called the worst financial crisis in history, what he meant by that. Remember at this time the world was in a real financial global meltdown. On the day of the interview Greece was very close to defaulting on its debt and the United Nations was the center of massive talks not only on global finances but the attempts by the Palestinians to forge a new state by United Nations decree.

"The American dream has been under assault for 30 years," said the former President. "I think the adoption of two bad ideas have accelerated it. First, we were gonna have challenges when we moved to a global financial system and an information technology revolution occurred which eliminated a lot of intermediate jobs and dramatically increased productivity. Then 35 years ago the idea of what a corporation is changed. Before then a corporation had more or less equal responsibilities to share-holders, its employees and its customers and the communities in which it supports. Now its share-holders up here (raised arm up high) and everyone else way down here (arm down low)."

Taken on its face Clinton and Gore knew the long-standing global model for business was going to go away and quickly. And with it would go millions of jobs. This was proven out very quickly once businesses realized they could move as much product on the web as they could in a stand alone store or through distributors. The web would take their products directly to the public who could use their credit cards on-line. PayPal and Google Checkout soon joined the fray making the transfer of money, without ever touching the filthy lucre, as easy as a click of a mouse.

Look where you pay your bills today. How many of us look at the checkbook and pay the bills on-line which are no longer delivered by your friendly neighborhood postman, but right to your email box. Two or three clicks later the money has left your bank account and is now in the possession and bank account of some multi-national, nameless, faceless corporation.

Looking for a book or a CD or a DVD? Where do you go? Amazon.com is the world's biggest retailer. Have you ever been to an Amazon store? Of course not because they don't exist and neither do employees for the most part. Amazon is really a conglomerate of small retailers and private sellers just like you or maybe your mom, who have something to sell and the channel is Amazon.com on the web.

Some of those sellers will offer new books versus used books. One may offer a new copy of the book for $29 despite the fact others are selling the same new book for $18. Another may offer the used copy at $8.43, another for $6.55 while still another who has just one copy and may be just a consumer with only one book period who is offering it for $2.50.

In 1970 for example if you wanted to buy a record album the way you went about it was simple. You went to a store, asked a clerk (employee) where the latest Beatles album was. He walked you over to the section where Beatles held sway. You then walked up to the register and handed it to a cashier (another employee) who then rang it up and put it in a bag.

Now how did it get there? The record company agent (employee) signed the Beatles, did all the publicity through their public relations department (employees), hired a producer (employee), printed the albums (employees), sales people (employees) sold them to distributors (employees) who then sold them to record stores (employees) who had the clerk (employee) stock the shelf, help you so you could buy it at the register from a cashier (employee) who would put it in a bag which was made by more people (employees). And don't forget the United States Postal Service who handled and delivered the mail and there would be about five stops along the way from the USPS.

No less than 15 different stops were made along the way from the singers to you walking out of the store with the merchandise. That is 15 different people who were employed by somebody and who had a job which they were paid to do. This does not count the redundancy in some of those departments so realistically there might be another 10 or 20 people involved but we will keep it simple.

Today a band decides to record a song. They get together with some quality programs on their computer and cut the song in their garage. They clean it up and make it sound really great on their computer. It may even be one singer using a program such as MXL Professional and creating all the music he needs on his home computer. I've done it myself and I'm not a musician. I did it for a video based on the Elvis song "Heart Break Hotel" which I put together to draw attention to the homeless.

Next the singer puts the song on YouTube for free and it goes all over the world. People download the song for free if they like it and maybe put it on their I-Pod or I-Phone. It went from singer to consumer directly and no one paid a dime for it. Oh it also bypassed at least 15 people who no longer have jobs because of this Internet delivery system. Oh, and nobody made a dime on it either.

The music industry isn't the only prime example. Every mom and pop retail store is affected by the Internet and the loss of jobs it creates. The Internet is not a job creator nor does it make things easier for people in business necessarily. It does improve efficiency because it cuts costs; employees specifically. If you don't need a distributor, a clerk, a cashier, a salesperson or anything more than a computer and a delivery system, why would you hire them?

Speaking of the US Postal Service, it is one of the great casualties of the World Wide Web explosion. The first segment of the USPS to feel the crunch was letter writing. With email which is free and instantaneous why on earth would you spend 44-cents to send a letter which takes five days to get to the person you sent it to? Only older people and those opposed to a computer would continue to write letters. By the year 2020 chances are most of them will be gone as may the local mailman. Both will have gone the way of the home delivery milkman. Some of you reading this today have no clue what a home delivery milkman is. Such is progress and the milkman went the way of the Dodo Bird without the Internet.

The USPS did have competition from Fed-Ex and United Parcel Service (UPS) and it did have a large union payroll but it served a purpose. Creator Ben Franklin might be rolling over in his grave at what has happened to the Post Office.

To its credit the USPS did strike a major partnership with eBay, chief among the internet job destroyers. It created a working relationship to make it easier for both eBay shoppers and eBay sellers to click and ship on the Internet thus making life more efficient. It even created Priority Mail Flat Rate to encourage shippers to use the post office and not the more reliable Fed-Ex or UPS. Things such as Delivery Confirmation and Package Tracking were big helps and credit was given to the Post Office for trying. Meanwhile the USPS started cutting jobs and in 2011 closed hundreds of facilities around the country to try to save itself. It also lost many long time employees and few new jobs were created. All in the name of efficiency and to try to save the institution.

This was only half of what the former president discussed in America's job creation scenario which was partially caused by the Internet.

"This 30 year anti-government rant America has been on, something no other country in the world is doing including ones that have been predominantly governed by conservatives in their country, instead of trying to figure out how government and private sector can work together saying that government is the source of all our problems if we just choked it off, there was never another regulation, never another tax, never another program, all would be well," said Bill Clinton. "There is not a single solitary example of that on the planet where that has worked. Including in America, it hasn't worked here."

At the time the Democrats led by President Barrack Obama were standing fast against the Republican majority in the US House of Representatives on entitlement programs and tax increases. Obama and House Speaker John Boehner were going toe to toe with the president finally drawing a line in the sand. His program for creating jobs was based on more stimulus money poured into the country, especially for the rebuilding of America's infrastructure. He was willing, against his own party's wishes, to make cuts to entitlement programs such as Social Security, if those cuts were offset by higher taxes placed on the wealthiest two percent of Americans.

Buoyed by comments from billionaire Warren Buffett that Buffett himself paid taxes at a lower rate than his own secretary, and Buffett calling for more taxes on billionaires such as himself, the President led a charge heading into the 2012 election season. He knew at this point whatever he did, or tried to do even if it was a GOP style agenda, the Republicans would oppose it based on trying to make Obama a one term president. So he drew the line in the sand putting the ball into GOP hands to try and persuade public opinion.

Clinton based much of his opinions on the reality of what was going on and that reality was finally sinking into Americans who understood the banks and the corporations were not hurting, they had the money and they just were not going to do anything with it. Clinton pointed out job growth was slow because first of all it takes time to get out of a recession. Historically, looking back about 400 years, the timing has pretty much always been a similar five-year cycle.

"I think because we just went through a financial crash and they generally take five years to get over," said Clinton in the Yahoo interview. "We still have a lot of detritus that hasn't been cleaned out from the housing crash. I think until we clean that up it's going to be hard to get bank lending going again even though the banks have more than $2 trillion uncommitted to loan, corporations have about that much they haven't invested and I think that what is uncertain is that demand. A lot of banks aren't making small business loans even where there is good compelling collateral. It's not because they are worried about regulations it's because they are earning a fair amount of money doing nothing, they don't have to pay any interest on deposits."

The Internet has made doing financial business, as Clinton stated above, easy. It really is a global financial system. In 1975 you had to get a wire transfer at a cost of $35 to send $350 from a bank in the United States to a bank in Italy. It might take 36 hours before it was confirmed. Today I can send $350 to a friend in Scotland in two seconds for free. Two seconds is the click of a mouse if I'm slow at the job. This is the beauty of the Internet. It is also a small job killer because instead of walking into the bank to get this done and have an employee process it at my end and at the other end in Scotland, two people at least were eliminated from the equation. These jobs, like the jobs above in the music industry are not coming back.

Clinton thinks things will return but in a different form. One thing which happened is something government has been telling Americans to do for decades; save.

"I think even in this economy savings has gone up among families because everybody is afraid," Clinton said. "Everybody sort of shuts down, as we clean up our financial books, including the government over the long run, and look at areas of real opportunity for job growth. I think we can get things going again."

So where does the Internet create new jobs? There are ways according to Clinton. First getting the housing market in order which does not involve the Web directly although the Web is used to buy, sell and rent homes all the time. More importantly the jobs are created through prosperity centers.

"There are dozens of other things you have to do starting with building on our successes. There are prosperity centers all over this country that are doing great. Silicon Valley is back, San Diego is the center of biotechnology in America and Pittsburgh is trying to become America's nanotechnology center. There are hundreds of computer simulation companies flourishing in Orlando," Clinton pointed out. "These prosperity clusters some people call them, they can be replicated throughout the country. They are all partnerships; they are totally different from the rhetoric of Washington. The government here the private sector here, everybody's fighting. They (prosperity centers) are all dominated by cooperation with everybody putting in what they are best at."

All of the above progress and business is transported on the Web in some way or fashion. It is the Web being useful in creating jobs and while they are different types of jobs – because as we stated earlier those other jobs are not coming back – these new jobs must be Web friendly. This also means increased efficiency which led the Internet job destruction and can now be used to create jobs although again these are different kinds of jobs.

Clinton called on both government and the private sector to reinvent themselves to work together especially in retrofitting public buildings.

“A system that would dramatically increase the rate at which we’re retrofitting government buildings, public schools, colleges and universities because it pays for itself. It is so easy and you are giving back cheap electricity to the power company which they can then sell back to new users at lower cost which helps to promote industrial use. I’d like to see us move more and more to a system where the big centralized power stations are used to power manufacturing and other big electricity uses and do it at a competitive rate because we can decentralize a lot of other things with small scale wind and solar technology and better efficiency.”

President Obama had been pushing for clean energy job creation almost from the beginning of his campaign. Clinton agrees while the GOP has always been skeptical of the story of Global Warming. It really hit home for the Republicans when former vice-president Al Gore won an Academy Award for his documentary “An Inconvenient Truth” about the warming of the earth’s atmosphere by Greenhouse gases.

“Al Gore has done yeoman’s work trying to educate people making movies and other people have done what they do,” Clinton said of his former running mate. “The great success of the anti-climate change crowd is to say there is no way to get rich, stay rich and get richer without putting more greenhouse gases in the atmosphere, the economy is in the dumps why in the world would we do this now. Let’s put it off and hope nothing bad happens to our kids. In other words it’s not that people don’t think it's real it's that 'I've got enough problems don't bother me with this.'"

The former leader of the free world said he looks at turning that around and doing something creative and positive.

"How can we make a dollar out of this, how can we prove this is good business, how can we put more people to work, how can we prove this is more labor intensive? I'll give you an example, an interesting study was done saying that if you change America's electric grid and use more solar and wind as opposed to using the same amount, use more nuclear and replace some of the inefficient coal with more efficient coal -- doing the clean energy alternative would create six-to-eight times as many jobs. Let's look at what creates jobs with the same power needs, and do what makes good economic sense, we want to put America back to work, create new jobs."

For him it is more of the argument you can catch more flies with honey than with vinegar.

"I figure that if we can prove that it will do more to save the planet than arguing about *how* to save the planet with people wondering where their next dollar is coming from."

Again it is all about efficiency and on a global scale.

"The older countries can create enormous numbers of jobs with a renewed round of efficiency commitments. The US is twice as energy efficient as we were during the first oil price embargo in the 1970s but we are more than twice as *inefficient* as a lot of our major competitors. We could literally create a million jobs here if we had a systematic way of financing building retrofits everywhere."

All of this does not count on the Internet but all the information, the transactions and much of the dialogue will travel on the Internet. The Internet, while being a major job destroyer, can be a major job creator if governments and private industry embrace a mutual set of goals to make it happen.

Positive Business on the Internet

No one would blame you the reader for reading the title of this chapter and looking ahead to see if indeed this is the shortest chapter in the book. Believe it or not there are positive things about business on the Internet. Actually there are many of them but not all businesses are suited to the Internet. There are some industries which will use the Internet to promote and drive customers to their standing business. As far as making money directly on the Internet there are not many. We will try to lay them out here.

It has often been said the most effective field of endeavor when it comes to business on the Internet is of course the auction industry. It may surprise you to read here that this is true. It won't surprise you to also read the auction business on the Internet has become so expansive it helps to ruin legitimate businesses under the legitimate business model we've been talking about. It has also become grossly oversaturated.

Of course eBay is the Cadillac of the auction business but it is by far not the only one. There are many legitimate auction houses which have taken themselves off the showroom floor and planted themselves squarely on the World Wide Web. The reason of course is first the low cost. The cost of doing business, as the title of this book states, is very low. Organizing a weekly auction, bringing items to the floor, hiring an auctioneer, doing the advertising and hoping people show up is not something which happens on the Internet.

The auction used to be a place of dealing and bidding and a night out on the town. People dressed up to go to Christies or Sotheby's or some of the other great auction houses. They would dress in coats and ties, they would have a numbered card to hold up and they would make strange little gestures to give the nod to the auctioneer to take the price to the next level.

With the Internet you could lie in your bed naked at three in the morning eating cookies and drinking milk and make a bid. Look it up on line, Google other auctions to get instant comparison pricing and then just "click" away. You might even subscribe to an auction sniper which automatically places your bid with three seconds remaining in the auction. However, I could never figure out who goes first if more than one auction sniper is playing the game in the same bidding war.

Auction sniping is another cottage industry which popped up with the Internet and is more closely linked to eBay than any other. Bulk listing companies were all the rage for a while. These companies developed software which allowed you to upload thousands of auctions to the web site at the same time. You still had to input them into the software individually of course but listing occurred at the same time allowing you to see the auctions end at the same time.

Now, back to the auctions themselves . There are more auctions on the Internet in one day than all the auctions before the Internet in a few decades. At any one time you can go to eBay and put in the name of a popular item in the Search engine and come up with 10,000 items. This is only one auction site. Less popular items appear less frequently.

In the sports card and memorabilia industry, which is highly populated with auctions you have Heritage, Memory Lane, Huggins and Scott, SPC, Goodwin and many more. The auction business has so saturated the industry it has forced the closure of more than 90-percent of the trading card shows in America. It has helped shut down hundreds of mom and pop hobby retail stores and has even hurt the price guide industry as well as the many grading services which help direct the industry.

With the closure of trading card shows and shops there has been a tremendous loss of advertising dollars to the once powerful Beckett Magazine. With the added loss of manufacturers, there is very little need to advertise in the Beckett publications and there is no need for the main reason the magazine existed in the first place; the price guide.

The average collector during the boom period waited weekly for the new "Beckett" (Beckett Magazine was a monthly card magazine dedicated to pricing and information about the industry) to arrive at his hobby store. Collectors and speculators wanted to see what their cards were worth today. Fewer and fewer stores even sell the price guides anymore. The reason is they can look on eBay or several other web sites for free and get instant pricing. Beckett formerly had its people call and go to hobby stores and shows (frequently called conventions) individually each month to get current pricing. This resulted in usually a three to four week delay in actual information flow.

They would survey stores as to what was selling and at what price. A less than scientific method to be sure but it was what was available and Dr. James Beckett, founder of the publication empire, became rich doing it. Dr. Beckett saw the Internet coming and sold out at the right time.

Today a customer walks into a hobby store and says "what is my Cal Ripken Rookie Card worth" and the dealer walks over to the computer, calls up eBay, puts *"Cal Ripken 1982"* into the search engine and immediately he sees what the card is selling for and what it has sold for in the last 30 days.

Who needs to spend $10 on an out-of-date price guide which was printed two weeks ago and researched a month ago? To add insult to injury who needs the card store when the collector could do the exact same thing at home at three in the morning lying naked in bed eating cookies and drinking milk? The Internet has done this.

How many jobs were lost due to this Internet phenomena? Beckett, the once powerful all American icon of the industry, now outsources customer service overseas. Price guide workers were laid off to compensate for the lack of sales and the Card Show Department which listed sports card conventions around the country is miniscule. The company is a shell of its former glory and constantly the subject of sale rumors. Much of Beckett now survives on its card grading service rather than its price guide and publication business.

There are even those who will take it a step farther.

"The National isn't what it used to be anymore," said collector/dealer Steve Wachsman in speaking of the National Sports Collectors Convention. "Dealers won't move on prices because they know they can get a higher price on the Internet than selling it cheap at the National Convention."

Wachsman is right. *The National* used to be the most awaited convention held each year in the industry. People would come from all over the world to visit the National. In 1991 alone, the highlight year, over 100,000 people attended the three day event in Anaheim, California. You couldn't move in the aisles on Saturday it was so crowded.

"Now you can roll a bowling ball down the aisle on Saturday afternoon and not hit anyone," added Wachsman. "Things certainly have changed."

It has gotten so bad The National now only is held in the Mid-western United States. This is where the hotbed of the hobby exists. From Cleveland to Chicago and the surrounding area commonly called "Chicagoland." Dealers won't allow it to go to Anaheim anymore and even Texas has been off limits. Dealers can't make enough money by traveling so far to do such a show. It is easier for them to say "come East and visit us," instead.

Again the Internet has had such an effect on this particular industry it has changed drastically and not for the better. The "better" is, more collectors are involved because they know they can complete their collections easier via the Internet than traveling to shows and stores around the country. Often they are willing to pay more to get those items. Most prefer to wait figuring they will eventually find it cheaper on the Internet and in the vast number of cases they do.

This is not to say those stores and dealers who have embraced the Internet are not succeeding. Many are. There are several stores around the country which have taken upwards of 90-percent of their sales on-line. Lower costs of course are the main reason plus walk-in traffic has virtually died. Others have adapted but the vast majority found it too difficult to compete with the lower prices on-line for their bread and butter sales, they just went away.

Even the auction companies are not immune to their own business making it very difficult to make and sustain a profit. Most auction houses have a few experts who travel the country following leads and getting consignments. These are paid employees or often work on commission as well as some base pay. Much of what the Internet auction house sells is consigned directly by the customer with no middleman and no payout aside from the person who consigned it.

One long time auction house has reps around the country who work on a commission basis only. The representatives get 10-percent of the hammer price of the auction for everything they acquire for consignment. The auction house also solicits and takes direct consignments from customers. The customer usually surrenders 15-percent to 20-percent of the sale price to the auction house of which the rep gets his 10-percent cut. This leaves the auction house with either five or 10 percent of the sale price. This barely covers expenses which include shipping, advertising and catalogs. This does not cover the many paid employees and the rest of the cost of doing business.

For instance, if an item sells for $200 the buyer will surrender 20-percent or $40 to the auction house. The representative gets $20 and the auction house gets $20. It will more often than not cost more than $20 to ship the item to the auction house in the first place and the auction house pays for the shipping. The auction house will charge the buyer 15-percent or in this case $30. Again this is not a lot and there may be only a dollar or two in the area known as profit. This is why an auction house will offer thousands of items each month or at each auction in hopes of selling it all and making a living.

Just about all auction houses also charge the buyer a premium of around 15-percent. It is out of this money the auction house actually pays employees, its bills and hopefully makes a profit. Often an on-line auction house will report sales of $5 million and there may have only been a few thousand dollars in profit. It is that tight and with more houses constantly coming on-line to take a cut of the action the profit margins are shrinking.

Another business which thrived in the early days of the Internet but which has now taken a big hit is the grading service part of the industry. PSA and BGS (A part of Beckett Media) have seen their numbers fall. These services basically rate the condition of trading cards and give them a number grade while placing them in an unbreakable (although dealers have found a way to break the holder without damaging the card but it can be tricky) holder. The practice is called "slabbing."

PSA and BGS are the two biggest. At one time there were about 20 such services of which several were bogus rip off artists capitalizing on the craze. They have since gone away.

A collector or dealer submits his card to PSA and PSA then examines the corners, the edges, the surface and the centering of the picture on the card. Each of these is weighted and the overall card is given a number from 1-10 with 10 being the highest. A grade of 10 is rare. Most vintage cards printed before 1970 will fall in the range of 4-7. Most brand new cards right out of the pack will register from 8-9.5. An older card say from 1960 with a 10 grade is so rare it could bring thousands of dollars at auction despite the fact the price guides list the "raw" card at about $4.

Grading really took off when the Internet moved into the auction state. In many cases a $4 card from 1963 would sell for as much as $100 if it was graded an 8 by PSA. PSA prints its population report and collectors and dealers could see why such a card gained so much value. There may have been a total of 5000 of that particular card graded with only a handful achieving PSA 8 status. It was truly rare.

Well really it wasn't *truly rare* it was just that so few had been graded. Ten years later the same card in a PSA 8 grade sells for about $10. The reason is simple. While ten years ago there were 5000 graded and only five PSA 8 cards, today there are 20,000 of the card graded and 200 in a PSA 8 grade. They are not that rare and the reason so many were sent in was the Internet explosion.

People saw the same $4 card they had in their collection was selling for $100. They sent it in for grading. Many came back less than 8 but a pretty strong number were graded 8 and some better. The population of PSA 8 cards went up and therefore demand for the card went down and so did the price. This only happened because of the Internet and the speed and hype which it brought.

So you ask yourself is the card really worth $4 or $100? If you say something is only worth what someone is willing to pay for it you are not exactly correct. Someone was willing to pay $100 for it then but only $10 now. Who do you believe? The price guides only reflect the latest selling price claiming they "are a guide only." The seller trying to sell it says it is worth $100, the dealer trying to buy it claims it is only worth $10. With the Internet you only have to wait for the price to come down and it will.

The other really good business on the Internet is best known by the name of the number one player in the industry; Google. Google is a verb as much as it is a noun. Google is synonymous with Search Engine. It is the most important item on the Internet because without the Search Engine how would you find anything?

Google started out as a laugh to many people. They constantly asked how on earth it could make money. It is one of the more expensive stocks on the stock market because it does make money and if we don't watch out will dominate the Internet even more than it does today.

As with Beckett in the trading card industry, Google is the major controller of information on the Internet. If you want to find something you "Google it." It is built into so many systems it is almost invaluable. There is competition from Microsoft with Bing and Yahoo, and DogPile and others but Google is the Cadillac of the Internet Search Engines.

It makes money for people and even has its own Email system called G-Mail. It has its own document system to compete with Word from Microsoft and it invades more places than the Norton Security System. It makes money with advertising and promoting advertising and clicks for higher placement for paying firms. Who doesn't want to be number one of the Google search list? Entire companies have been developed on the Web which do nothing but try to get your company web site placed higher and higher in the searches.

In 2011 Google unveiled a social networking system to compete with FaceBook. This came just a few weeks after Google shelled out $12 billion in cash for Motorola. Google perhaps is one of the most powerful companies on the Web.

To show you how important a well maintained web search is here is an example. A company I worked for highly promoted its website for about two years. During that time it had a full time web person in-house working daily to promote the website with updates. The company sent out news flashes directing people to the website hourly.

Every time I Googled my own name, "Bob Brill," this particular company with my name came up number one. Every time without exception I was number one because of this company website. This was despite the presence of many well known Bob Brill's who were doing much more than I was to promote my own name.

An Intellectual Properties attorney in Chicago by the name of Bob Brill works very aggressively at promoting his business and himself. We never found him any higher than number two during this time. Other famous Bob Brill's would also pop up along with other items featuring me such as books and Blogs I was writing.

Then for some reason the corporate executives of the company I worked for decided to change the way the website was run and took it out of the hands of the local divisions around the country. After about 30 days I did the same Google test for Bob Brill. Not only was I no longer number one but my ranking for this particular company fell to no. 71! In fact, before I came up on the company site I popped up for other things I had done over the years. Several times the Bob Brill which came up on the search engine was something I had done five years previously.

If nothing else this shows the importance of keeping up a web presence once you have one. Was the change in the way the company promoted the website a mistake? It was for many reasons but whether corporate actually saved any money doing it is a question only they and the stockholders can answer.

As mentioned earlier there are other positive new businesses on the Internet. Companies such as those who do Internet Marketing have sprung up all over. But with so many of them using the same techniques they aren't very different. Beware of those firms which promise to put you in the top ten searches in all the search engines.

Another Internet exclusive cottage part of the industry is the email submitter. You receive so much "Spam" in your email box most of us have strong filters to keep the spam from coming in. We might lose a good email once in a while but it is okay considering the thousands of spam per day we could be getting. Firms such as Constant Contact work to get our bulk messages out to people who want to read what we have to say. Bloggers, newsletter writers, clients and customers really do want to stay in touch with us and for a small fee a company such as Constant Contact sends out those emails for us with links to what we want our readers to see.

For as little as $15 a month we can send thousands of emails to fans and clients and we are pretty much assured they will go through not as SPAM but as legitimate emails. The reports tell us what percentage of these emails were received, read and followed up on by going to the link we provided. It even tells us who "opted out" because they don't want to hear from us. All of this at the click of the mouse and all of it invaluable in our email marketing campaign.

Now as previously mentioned this is done at a very low price and how any company can survive by charging $15 a month even in volumes of a thousand or more, boggles the mind. Then again once the system is set up there isn't much to do except to market for new clients. That is until another company comes along and offers the same service for $10 a month and it will. Why? Simply, because it is the Internet.

At some point some well heeled larger Internet company will offer it as a free service and the Constant Contacts of the world will be gone. Google could do this in a heartbeat. It might even buy a firm such as Constant Contact and incorporate it into its own system for free.

"The Internet is all about change," said Dave Rodriguez, who runs Signatures.com. "You have to keep changing with it; it's always going to change to stay fresh."

Rodriguez should know. He has been in the website business since the beginning of the Internet. At the moment his web address (signatures.com) might be more valuable than the business he runs on it. Selling Internet addresses is another business exclusive to the Web itself.

At some point along the way someone figured out they could make money by registering every possible domain name which sounded catchy. After all it cost less than $5 to secure a web address. If you owned the right one and someday someone decided they HAD to have that name you could sell it to them for a hefty price.

Web Domain company "GoDaddy.com" offers domain name auctions constantly on the site. There again is that word "auction."

At one point the name of NBA superstar Michael Jordan had dozens of variations with buyers hoping to capitalize on Jordan's name. If his company wanted to buy any of these the seller figured they could make a bundle. There was MichaelJordan.com, MJ.com, MJNBA.com, MichaelJordanNBA.com and on and on. One of the most recent phenomena has been the selling of the original name of the social networking site; Facebook.

The original name used by Mark Zuckerberg when he put his idea into action was "Facemash." It sold at auction for just over $30,000. Facebook and its entire social networking prowess basically replaced email for younger users. Begun in 2004, by 2011 it had 500 million users worldwide with revenues of $800 million. Let me repeat this; $800 million. Banner ads, advertising on the site and little else are where the money comes from because Facebook is FREE! It costs nothing to participate, play games, and stay in contact with friends or just chat. It is FREE. There is that word again.

What does Facebook do? It allows you to have a community of friends who post to your "Wall" instantly. It allows you to play any of the many licensed Facebook games on line with your friends such as "Animal Farm" and "Mafia Wars" to name just two. You can "Poke" your friends or send them virtual flowers.

Even the Queen of England has her own Facebook page. However, the Royal cannot be "friended" on the site. You can check out her schedule on Facebook and millions have. Any public information about the Queen that Buckingham Palace wants put out there will likely be seen on the social networking site.

"Social Networking," as it has been dubbed, has been around since the beginning of the Internet. It went from chat boards to email, to My Space and the video social networking site; YouTube. My Space died when Facebook took off. There are others of smaller means. Twitter added the word Tweet to our vocabulary.

What is Twitter? Twitter is a means of using up to 140 characters to let your friends and "followers" know what is going on in your life. Want to let them know you will be in Amarillo, Texas for the weekend? Send out a Tweet. Want to let them know you have a cold? Send out a Tweet. Want to let them know you are in the bathroom reading the latest copy of WE Magazine? Send out a Tweet.

When Jack Dorsey created Twitter in 2006 he probably didn't have any idea by 2011 there would be 175 million users of Twitter. It is sometimes thought of as "microblogging" which means basically letting someone have a small bit of information. The wider use of texting so to speak.

Does Twitter make money? You would think so but it isn't easy. How does one advertise? Google may pick this one up as well as you can offer this service for free just as Facebook is free. The website "did you ever wonder" has the best explanation we've seen:

"All tweets are searchable on the website, and they feature in the search results of Google, Bing, and Yahoo search engines. Hint hint – Yes, Twitter sells its tweets related to a particular topic to these search engines, and that's one way of making money. Twitter sells the rights to publish live tweets on any hot, trending topic (for example, the Football world cup, or The Royal Wedding of William and Kate). Search engines get live data and unique comments through each tweet. As a by-product, Twitter gets more users. An ideal win-win situation!

Another money-generating model is to show "Promoted Tweets". Advertisers pay Twitter to show their tweets in top search results, along with their company name. Likewise, there are "Promoted Trends" where How Does Twitter Make Money? The advertiser's product related trends are featured on the website. Major companies like Coca Cola, Starbucks, and Disney have already made deals with Twitter to promote their products."

There are other social networking sites and more will come and go as the Web grows. To say Facebook has replaced email is a bold statement but it is pretty much true. Consultant Victor Shaffer was at a Las Vegas seminar when he asked the audience how many of them had kids who were about 15 years old.

About half the room raised their hands.

"How many of them communicate with email?" The consultant asked.

About four or five kept their hands up.

"Those are pretty much old school teenagers," Shaffer responded. "Today kids use email like we used fax machines."

Shaffer went on to explain how the youth of the world did two things more than anything else. They communicated on the Web via Facebook and Twitter and they communicated on their cell phones via Text rather than talking. The downside of course there was no longer a face to face chat or meeting or a handshake or anything else which involved eye to eye trust. All that was out there was a marketplace. This marketplace was reachable instantly and without too much cost. Almost no cost or no barrier to entry.

The Internet has created this vast way of instant communications which has moved the youth of the world and the growing older youth into a place where their parents had never gone. By 2010 there were still people in the world who did not have access to a computer and the Web but they were getting older and falling by the wayside somewhat rapidly.

I decided to contact a distant cousin in Italy. Pina is in her 60's and I knew she did not have a computer. I found her doing family research in the city of Potenza where my paternal grandparents had migrated from in 1896. I had not spoken with her in 10 years and decided it was time to reconnect.

I sat down at my computer and went to Google Translate on the Web and wrote her a three page letter. It instantly translated to proper Italian, I printed it out and sent the letter to her via the US Postal Service.

Ten days later I received a letter in the mail from Pina. It was handwritten and very difficult to read. I tried to put it into Google Translate and after a lot of deciphering two days later I had it pretty much figured out. One of the lines in the letter stated she "did not have email" but she would "contact her nephew" who did have email so we could communicate. I too communicate with him now via email and Facebook.

Imagine how much easier it would have been if she had access to a computer and was able to go on-line. There are several young women in the same town who are the daughters of my best friend (he has since passed away) with whom I communicate often on Facebook. Occasionally I also get an email but almost always it is on Facebook where I communicate with these 30-something young ladies. Yes, when it comes to communication the Internet is a wonderful thing.

Speaking of which let me ask if you ever tried on-line dating. There are far too many sites involved in hooking people up to begin to mention but I'll deal with a few. First let me say if you are single you probably have at least considered dating on line. It doesn't stop there however as there are sites for people who are married and looking for outside encounters of almost every kind. We know from the FBI busts there are also illegal networks of child pornographers using the Web exclusively as predators to harm children. There are also Gay sites catering to homosexuals, Christian sites working with believers of certain denominations of the Christian religion, Jewish sites, Persian sites and so on.

Internet dating started out on a pay by credit card basis. One of the earliest and most successful has been eHarmony.com. The founders of this site advertise on television and radio constantly and charge you a monthly fee for their service. There are different levels depending on how much of their advice and help you want in seeking out potential mates. eHarmony did a good amount of business and was going very well but the owners had to figure at some point what they were offering for a fee someone was eventually going to offer for FREE. Yep there is that word again.

There are dozens of free sites to choose from. There is OKCupid.com, PlentyofFish.com, Match.com and too many others to mention. Both OKCupid and PlentyofFish offer their basic service without charging you. You must register and there are certain profiles you need to fill out but basically the service is free. There is an "upgraded" service which you can purchase on both for a small monthly fee but only if you want their help in finding a date or a mate. If you feel confident on your own of your own abilities then charge on.

These sites base themselves on matching your personality and profile and your wants and desires with someone who has many of the same personality traits and wants and desires as you. One site offers a thousand questions for you to answer and you can answer as many as you like. The more you answer the more narrow the search gets for your future companion.

Another site offers a chance for you to put more photos on the site while one will restrict your photos to only current day pictures of yourself. I tried putting some childhood photos of me on one site because people said they were "cute."The site managers took them down. Darn.

Security should be and often is a high priority on dating sites. A woman sued Match.com after she was assaulted by a man she met on the site. Turns out the guy had a criminal record. The woman didn't want any money but did want Match.com to somehow run security checks against state and federal predator lists before letting people on the site. The website operators gave in much to their credit. All dating sites should have some security.

The way the sites mostly work is they of course let you post photos of yourself up front. The basic feeling is who wants to date someone you are not attracted to. Due to this you can ask any pretty woman how many "hits" they get from prospective suitors. It's a proven fact good looking people have a better chance to get the job than non-attractive people. The same goes for Internet dating. Even those who have no chance at dating that woman who looks like a super model will try to contact them figuring nothing ventured nothing gained. Like hitting on a great looking woman at a bar you can figure you are out of luck on-line too.

The sites also offer a chance for you to fill in the blanks when it comes to age (to which a huge percentage of people lie), height, weight, job description, salary, kids or do you want kids, hair color, eyes and anything else you can think of when making a list of things you want in a potential mate including religious affiliation. Many of these are optional of course while others are mandatory.

Then you type certain items into a search engine and begin looking. You can also just let the site computer send you "matches" or people who fit the description of what you want and hopefully you are what they are looking for.

Internet dating flourishes on the Web and it has for the most part replaced the bars as a place to meet potential mates. Once you find someone you are attracted to you can communicate via email. You can then set up a meet, a coffee-date or an outing. Coffee-dates are all the rage and Starbucks and Coffee Bean & Tea Leaf, love it. Starbucks has really replaced the local bar for hooking up so to speak.

Eventually Web based dating will pretty much replace all other forms of dating. It is strictly a numbers game and those who play it, know it as exactly that. It is also fun. In the case of eHarmony.com they take a little different tackand are probably more concerned with security than most other sites. Your first option is not directly emailing someone you are interested in. They have a series of ice-breakers you usually try first to gauge the interest of the other person who as soon as they see the message they will check out your photo and profile. Then and only then will they decide to respond. Often they do not. It is still a numbers game and once you get started you are on your own just as if you had met in a bar, a club, a church or were introduced by a family friend.

It must be said here the Internet has vastly improved the chances of millions of people around the world of finding their soul mate. It has also increased the chances a sexual predator will find another prey whether it is a child, a woman or via a Gay relationship. The FBI files are filled with thousands if not millions of names who have preyed on victims via Internet social networking sites. It has made finding your love easier but it's also led to the rapes and murders of thousands worldwide.

Awful Business on the Internet

Since the Internet is all about writing you might think the Internet would spur on reading good books and getting great books published. Not so cowboy, in fact, the Internet has practically killed the publishing business and all the jobs which it supports. It has also created some new opportunities but at lower pay levels and as is usually the case with the Internet, more output with lower margins of profit.

Ask an agent how much he used to make as compared to what he makes today. Ask an author how much he used to make and what he makes today. Seeking a job in publishing? You will hear how the market is not only shrinking but the jobs that are left are going away as well.

A New York Times runaway best seller is still a New York Times runaway best seller but they are fewer, and far and away less profitable than before the Internet. Today a huge number of Vanity presses or self publishing houses have popped up. These are companies who, for a fee which you pay them, will publish your book. They will set you up with a cheapie web site as a place to market your book, they will send you a certain number of copies of your book for you to sell (especially at book signings that you set up) and they will pay you half the royalties on sales.

They offer really no financial support at all and every dime you spend on promoting your book comes out of your pocket. The websites they set up for you? You can find these for as little as $5 on-line and in many cases such inexpensive websites, which do offer a shopping cart for sales and PayPal as a credit card taker, can be had for FREE. There is that word again. So when the vanity publisher tells you he's giving you this great website "a $300 value," they are really just giving you something they aren't paying for in the first place.

Now get out and start calling those bookstores to see which ones will place your book. That is extremely difficult because they don't want the accounting nightmare, they don't have the space and there is no marketing dollars behind your book which will push sales. The bookstore, which also sells virtually as well as at a storefront, must make a profit. There is that word again as well; PROFIT.

You might be able to get them to let you sign copies of your book and give a talk at their local store. This is not as easy as it sounds either. You are virtually an unknown, with no marketing behind your book and you are hoping to get 20 people out to visit with you and maybe some will buy your book through the bookstore which will handle the sales.

"Do you have a list of relatives and friends you can get to come out for your signing?" This is a common question the bookstore owner/marketing person will ask you.

Of course these are your friends who support you and you've already given them a book in the first place. Why would they buy another one because you are signing at Barnes and Noble? They won't.

So there you are. You just spent $1000 to get your book published. You have 250 copies of the book in the trunk of your car, 25 of which will go to friends and a few to people like your local newspaper, radio and television station as "Review Copies." These you just give away. You will get emails from Internet Radio hosts who will want a copy of the book to do an interview with you on their show. Few people listen to these programs but it is a chance to get your name out there and be heard and it costs nothing but a book and postage.

The good thing is you have your name on a book and someone somewhere will buy it and along the way copies will get passed on and picked up at garage sales and you will be remembered by someone. You also have the good feeling you can now say "I am an author." Occasionally someone likes the book enough to offer you a real contract to publish the book and even movie deals do come along. These are few and far between but they do happen.

Chris Madsen is a sportscaster in Los Angeles and a big time player. Madsen was the voice of the Anaheim Ducks of the NHL and an award winning announcer. Chris had no luck finding an agent or a publisher and finally with his partner decided to self-publish the book they wrote.

Madsen's critically acclaimed book "Joshua Shoots! He Scores!" *The Greatest Call I Ever Made*, has benefited numerous charities, schools and organizations. It is the heartwarming story of Chris's relationship with an aspiring young broadcaster, Joshua Souder, challenged by Cerebral Palsy.

The book was seen by an agent who loved it, got it published by a real publishing house and the rights were later sold for the book to become a film. It does happen. Chris has his own company, Madsen Media and covers a lot of bases including as an inspirational speaker. Chris was one of the lucky ones in the publishing scenario.

Publishing was challenged greatly by the Internet which soon found major firms, even bookstore firms, competing for the rights to sell virtual books. The Kindle is one of many devices on the market where readers can download an e-book (the virtual version of the paper book) and for a much smaller price. They can read it on the device which they can carry around, on a trip, read on an airplane, etc. It is the way things are going. It was estimated by 2009 about 4% of book sales were e-books. It is the fastest growing segment of the publishing universe.

Why not you ask? Aren't newspapers folding left and right and going on-line? We'll get to those later and the jobs lost and the journalism sacrificed.

It is true the virtual world will be the next plain to cross and e-books are still finding their way. With the push to save trees you would think more people would be embracing this. Truth is most book readers like the feel of a real book. They like the smell of a real book and they like to bend the corner to mark the spot where they left off. They like to hold the book with one hand and eat chips with the other.

"There is something about a book in your hand you can't get from a computer device," my sister June once told me.

She is right. However we are talking business here and books are business. E-commerce is business and books will eventually go away for the most part. Getting good books made is another story. You see authors must get paid. Seeing your name on a book doesn't put food on the table and you can't spend your book at the A&P. With the virtual world closing in on the retail store, the retail price of a hard cover book may be $29.99. You can buy it on Amazon for about $19 or less. The virtual version will cost you, in 2011 dollars, $2.99.

Unless you are a recognized best-selling author, as an author you usually get 10%-15% of the wholesale price of the book. The wholesale price is on average about 50% of the suggested retail price of the book. It varies from company to company and from author deal to author deal but 50% is a nice rule of thumb and one we will use here.

So if the book sells for $30 and the wholesale price of the book is $15 and the author gets 15% of the wholesale price, he is now getting $2.25 per book. This is not a lot of money. This again is for just a standard novel or non-fiction book with no advance payment to the author.

Now take the virtual book which is going to sell for $3.00. Since there is no real cost to producing the book the author is now given a percentage of the sale. If you offered them 15% as you did with the hard cover version you would be paying them 45-cents per downloaded book. You can see where this is going.

So companies such as Amazon and E-Reads have to offer more than such a low percentage. At one point Amazon talked about offering 70% of the sale price to self published authors as a way to lure them into the Amazon fold. Best sellers were to be sold at $9.99 and any e-book had to be sold at least 20% lower than the list price of the physical book. Again you can see where this is going. Offering hard covers of best-sellers so cheaply gives the public the impression the book is only worth $10. Also by selling the e-book for let's say 60% of the best seller price (or $6.00) and giving the author 70-percent of the sale (about $3.75) the author makes a little more money. Of course the e-book virtually (no pun intended) costs the publisher zero dollars to make. One e-book can be downloaded forever after the initial cost of placing it on a web site which again is basically costing the publisher zero dollars.

Basically the publisher will find the competition greater than first anticipated and drop the cost of the e-book to perhaps $3 to make more sales. Since it cost virtually zero dollars to produce over and over again, the end result is everyone, including the author, will make less money. This, by the way, is on a "best-seller." No telling what the seller will sell the rest of the books for and how little the authors will get paid for their work. Many of these authors sell their books for only 99-cents! They get a lower percentage of the sale. They get about $.35 per book sold.

Here we go again with the Internet giving the impression you must give it away to be successful. Rather than increasing the price of physical books and using the excuse that trees are in short supply the Internet is forcing business people to go the other way. Less profit will be made and fewer dollars going to writers to make a living at their craft.

If you look at the above scenario, yes, it does point out the authors will actually make more physical dollars per book on e-books. Will more e-books be sold than physical books? What other restrictions will the specific company place on authors selling their books in this manner? When will the payment structure change to a lower point because the large company isn't make enough of a profit on e-books? And what about those slow selling books not on the New York Times Best Seller List? Will the pay to those other authors be only 20-percent instead of 70%?

It gets even worse if you take the tack Random House was looking at taking as late as August, 2010 with royalties for e-book starting at 25% and capping at 40%. Do the math on this one and you see why authors know they need to embrace e-books but aren't too thrilled about it.

Then there is the advance. Typically a new author signing with a major publishing house could have expected an advance on royalties in the low six figures. A $100,000 payment was not out of the question and then once the sales got to a certain point the author was paid a percentage of book sales. Typically today this has changed to the point where a new author might get an advance of about $15,000 for the same book and a lower amount on percentage of e-books sold. For a craft which deals with 99% rejection as a general way of life, this is not encouraging and does not encourage the free flow of ideas by writers. This is the ethical part of the industry we won't even begin to touch here.

Behind the scenes the numbers are dwindling due to the trickle down effect of the Internet. There is less of a desire to hire editors, spell checkers, fact checkers and general support personnel. With sales of physical books down and the income from e-books marginal there is little desire to hire support staff and certainly not at good wages. Interns are still cheap and easy to get. Well paid and good editors are being replaced by lower paid kids right out of school.

Blame Spell Check for a portion of it. While it does make the writer's job easier it is a two edged sword. It cost someone a job.

What the Internet has caused is the free flow of ideas through blogging. Blogging began with housewives telling about their daily agenda. It gave grandma the chance to see what little Jimmy was doing today.

A blog from mom might be 200 words on what her day was like and when the two year old went "poo-poo in the big toilet." Today the Blog has become a noun and a verb. The most prominent people in the world write daily blogs and so do many lesser known persons. The free flow of ideas is critical in a Democratic/Republic society. The blog is good for this. It is not good when it replaces good, solid and well trained journalists who make their living reporting the facts. While they too have *had* to become bloggers by their bosses they are being sacrificed for the expediency of the Internet and not even for e-commerce.

A perfect example is "The Brill Report." The Brill Report began as a Fax Newsletter highlighting the business end of a specific industry. I wrote it from my home computer and charged $40 per month to subscribe. If you bought it for a year in advance you were given a 13th month free of charge. It was a nice and easy marketing tool of which many customers took advantage. It gave me some operating capital and the security of knowing I'd be doing this and making a living at it for a year in advance.

Eventually choices had to be made and as successful as it was I sold The Brill Report for a nice profit and moved on. Years later I was encouraged to bring it back on the Internet. I resisted for several years knowing, with fewer corporate customers in the industry, the money wasn't going to be there. In addition, I knew no one believed they should pay for anything on the Internet.

The times changed and with lots of encouragement I restarted TBR as an on-line newsletter. People began calling it a blog. It was vastly improved and was colorful with photos, links to other sites and stories and was a really well put together project. I charged $5 a month for the subscription. I got a total of six subscribers after about six months.

I even got an email from a guy who stated "Why would I ever pay for this information?" I laughed because I got the same question posed to me about the original Fax TBR by an executive I knew at a corporation. Within three months that executive had his own personal subscription as did five others in his company including the president. I was making $200 per month from this one company. The man on the Internet was asking the same question and it wasn't long before I realized the on-line TBR had to be free and maybe advertising could be sold.

It went free and immediately was drawing good strong numbers of readers. Hundreds were reading it right away according to the reports I got from my site charts. Advertising however was non-existent and with a shrinking corporate base in the industry eventually The Brill Report, despite strong readership, went on hiatus and finally just stopped. I had to give it up and I didn't mind. The effort and the time and the expense of gathering the news, checking it out thoroughly and making sure it was correct, was too costly and time consuming. It was over because it was the Internet.

In 2011 the Newsletter (blog) LA Radio People had the same experience. The newsletter was a niche blog focusing on people who worked in radio in Los Angeles. It was well written by Don Barrett and a few contributors. It was informative and highly regarded by most people in the market. The publisher realized however it had to be free or die. It went away after never really attracting the advertising base needed to support its publisher.

Despite strong readership the niche market of the report just wasn't impressive enough to those who would pay to keep it going. He too was charging less than $5 per month. As with The Brill Report he also found people would forward the newsletter on to other non-paying readers. So while with both publications, there were more readers than we knew about, there was very little income. There certainly was not enough to support publishing.

Now fast forward to today. Everyone is a blogger reporting "news" as they see fit. Bill Maher made a great point on his "Real Time" show on HBO in November, 2010. He pointed out some blogger in India, where President Obama was traveling at the time; reported Mr. Obama's trip was costing $200 million a day. It is a figure which was denied and was totally incorrect. It was incorrect to even fathom the total if you look at the trip and the entourage going with the President.

The problem was other bloggers picked it up, commentators ran with it and a few legitimate news organizations reported it. Nearly all reported it as "rumored" and eventually denied. They also eventually reported it came from a blogger on the Internet. The Internet, with its no barrier to entry and lack of controls had done it again. Every time something like this happens it raises the hairs on the back of the neck of legitimate journalists. Not only is it damaging to legitimate news sources and outlets but it is economically damaging to business.

While working at United Press International and working on the Business desk out of Los Angeles one day we heard a rumor was circulating that Charles Schwab, the well known and very powerful, Wall Street stockbroker was selling his company. I immediately called Schwab's media contact to follow up the rumor. The man denied the report to me and that was good enough for me at the time.

Ten minutes later I received a second call. This time from Charles Schwab himself. He wanted first for me to know there was no truth to the rumor, second he wanted to know where I heard it and third he wanted to emphasize to me that even reporting this story as a rumor being denied would greatly damage tens of thousands of people. His entire client base would be affected along with his company and thousands of others on Wall Street who might make the wrong decisions based on such bogus information.

Since there were no further reports anywhere else about the rumor and there seemed to be nothing to it we made the decision to not even report the fact Schwab himself called to deny the rumor. It turned out to be just a rumor and nothing more.

We did the responsible thing and no one was hurt. Today even a responsible journalist might report the rumor being denied. An Internet blogger would very likely report the rumor and perhaps even report it as truth. What recourse would Schwab have? All this would be done to what purpose? The purpose was drawing attention to the blogger or the news outlet and nothing else. There was no legitimate reason for reporting this at all.

Schwab could sue the blogger who might turn out to be some kid on the Internet or even some retired pensioner living month-to-month. Why waste the legal costs to sue them. It might have been some 20-something trying to be sarcastic and fancying himself a great opinionater. Or it could have been anyone from a disgruntled stockholder to a person who just wanted to make a name for himself. In any case not someone Schwab would relish going after legally.

There are any number of examples we could put here regarding the use of the Internet as a way to destroy a person's reputation or livelihood. The stories are endless and the bottom line is what it has done to true, hardworking and well trained journalists. Not to mention these journalists are now required to write blogs for their companies in many, many cases.

Let's go back in time to the early 1970's when Richard Nixon was in office. There was a break-in at the Watergate building which was really insignificant at the time. Within days however it was learned the Watergate burglars did so under the guise of Republican operatives performing dirty tricks.

Two enterprising reporters, young reporters but well trained were assigned to the story. Bob Woodward and Carl Bernstein worked for the Washington Post under then editor Ben Bradley. Bradley was an old war horse as was his team of senior editors who laid out the paper every day. Bradley knew something about not getting sued because he wanted you to get the story right and insisted you didn't run with the story until you got the facts straight.

Woodward and Bernstein came up with a lot of good "possibilities" regarding the story and how high up what was eventually a cover-up, really went. We all know in hindsight it stopped at Nixon who got involved in and essentially approved the illegal cover-up of the crime. It led to his demise and he became the only president in American history to resign from office.

Can you imagine if this took place today? Within five minutes of getting a whiff of the story, a possible White House connection via the Committee to Re-Elect the President (CREEP) some blogger would have released the story with lots of opinions and hypothesis and blown the actual story. Nixon and crew would have had the time to effect a really big cover up of the cover up.

Legitimate reporters such as Woodward, Bernstein and even Bradley would never had the impact they had with their story had a blogger released it first. Within days or even hours other blogs around the world would have jumped on the lead and none of us would have ever known the real truth.

There are those who state categorically that because of the massive number of bloggers more stories get attention which would never be covered by the legitimate news media. There is some truth to this but the important stories, the stories which matter most to the world must be covered with facts, not innuendo.

If something is clearly opinion, or tongue in cheek, it is quite a different story. What passes for news however is what bloggers constantly write and get away with as legitimate news. The reason is of course there is No Barrier to Entry. Anyone can own a website, as previously stated, for $5 or even Free. Once you have this website you can write whatever you want. You can publicize it very quickly and through RSS Feeds, Google, Constant Contact and any other inexpensive or free means, get your opinions to be read by thousands of people daily. If you are good at it or just lucky or maybe just controversial you can affect the lives of millions of people.

If you are outrageous enough you will even get comments and responses which will only increase your Google rankings and more people will read what you have written.

You could very easily write something such as the following:

"Former Presidential Candidate John Edwards denies he is Gay."

Then cite your own "sources" which may or may not exist and by using Edwards' history of philandering as a backdrop, make all sorts of innuendos leaving the conclusion as to his alleged bi-sexual life up to the readers.

Such a headline alone would cause a stir and people would read it just to find out what it says. This would lead to more people reading it and before long, perhaps within only days or hours news agencies would pick up the story and someone would confront Edwards about the situation. Of course he would deny he was Gay and the blogger would gloat leading him/her to write more outrageous stuff.

It didn't matter the original story was a figment of the blogger's imagination and they were just sensationalizing and capitalizing on what has become a horrible situation for the former lawmaker and his family. Granted it was at his doing but where does it stop? When does the blogger smear someone who hasn't done anything to deserve public outrage? When does the blogger face the consequences of his actions and when does some control somewhere stop the blogger from ruining lives for fun.

Remember too, the blogger isn't getting paid to do this and there is no advertising involved so its all about their own ego. No barrier and no profit? This sounds like a case made for the Internet. It is.

The trickle down effect of publishing and the Internet has cost thousands of jobs in the field of journalism. Where once mighty newspapers stood with scores of reporters covering every beat possible, the Internet covers the same ground although not as well, with a handful of reporters.

In the early 1980's United Press International, one of the three major wire services and the only one never to legitimately financially sustain itself, was sold by the Scripps newspaper company for $1.00 to a pair of Tennessee rich boys (Douglas Ruhe and William Geissler) who wanted to own a news operation. While making cuts they ran up horrendous bills while traveling in style on the company dime. At one point this now bankrupt news agency and a mighty bastion of legitimate news, along with the Associated Press and Reuters, was $24 million in debt and losing about $2 million a month.

UPI had several suitors from all over the world. The staff was very wary of any foreign investment as were media watchers. UPI had long been an American company covering the world and well respected despite never making money and being subsidized by Scripps. It was the merger of United Press and Hearst's International News Service which brought the 1980's version of UPI to the stage at that time.

When afternoon newspapers began to fall by the wayside, Scripps decided it could no longer subsidize the wire service and then unloaded it for the princely sum of $1.00. Now however it was coming down to the last minute and UPI staffers around the world were bailing out of the respected news organization.

Earlier in the process evangelist Pat Robertson, himself a well known radio preacher, decided to make an offer for the company. He was seriously interested in the UPI Radio Network which for many years had been one of the few profit making centers of UPI. Robertson made what most down-holders (former UPI Staff members) considered a ridiculous offer for the company. The offer appeared legitimate and Robertson and his team of accountants made their way to UPI World Wide Headquarters in Washington, D.C. to go over the books.

A couple of weeks went by and it was announced Robertson had pulled out. The official statement went something like after looking over UPI's financial situation the purchaser felt it was too much money to pour into the company to get it operating again at a profit. So Robertson left and the pursuit for a buyer went on.

Curiously though soon after Robertson's offer was pulled back many of the stations in the UPI Radio Network (the company had nearly every religious station in the country in the network) began to cancel or not renew their contracts. They were however going over to a new network of religious stations Robertson's company was promoting. The suggestion around the company was that Robertson made the offer to look at the books and then steal the client stations away from UPI. Whether this was his intent or not it was a result few employees at UPI wanted to ignore.

The savior came in the form of a Mexican Newspaper magnate by the name of Mario Vazquez-Rana. He was the brother-in-law of former Mexican President Luis Echeverria, who was a close ally of Cuban President Fidel Castro. This scenario didn't wash at all with the employees or management although management was getting close to jumping off a bridge if someone didn't buy the dying news service. Vazquez-Rana also served on the Mexican Olympic Committee and was a well respected person in Latin America. He was also the equivalent at the time of a billionaire.

As the head of the board of directors of Organizacion Editorial Mexicana he was the head of the largest newspaper organization in Latin America. At the time in Mexico the ties with the ruling party in Mexico City and the newspapers were based on politics and somewhat on who paid whom. The government then, controlled newsprint. So, if a newspaper were to exist it needed to stay in good stead with the ruling party. Having the president as your brother-in-law was a pretty good thing to have. Even after Echeverria lost power, Vazquez-Rana held sway in the world of journalism with his more clean ties to sports and being well known internationally.

He was offering to buy UPI, pay off all its debts and get it running again. UPI was very big in Latin America as well as Asia. UPI was the most respected news service in both places while AP held court pretty much everywhere else and Reuters was very strong in Europe. The Reverend Sun Myung Moon also wanted UPI. The staff threatened to quit if the head of the Unification Church (commonly called the Moonies) got the company. No one wanted the Mexican newspaper owner but they knew he had the money to buy it. A deal was cut with a Texas real estate developer who also wanted the company so that the Texan became a partner in what amounted to name only.

That settled, Vazquez-Rana became the new owner of UPI. The man's first day on the job he was in for a rude awakening. In Mexico the newspaper union was owned by the company. Sure they discussed what was going to be in the contract but it amounted to little more than the company saying "this is what we are going to give you" and the union saying "okay."

The employees balked and while Vazquez-Rana was writing out the checks to creditors he must have been wondering to himself what in the world had he gotten himself into. For nearly three years the relationship was tentative but the company was working again and was doing good things. Vazquez-Rana for his part was throwing money down a rat hole. After nearly three years and $24 million (conservative estimate reported) the Mexican had had enough. He was pulling the plug.

Again the company was handed over to some not very trust worthy individuals. Dr. Earl Brian was a former member of Ronald Reagan's Kitchen Cabinet during his term as Governor of California and the-then head of FNN or the Financial News Network. Along with his business entourage of investors they took UPI off of Vazquez-Rana's hands and quickly sent it into a tailspin.

On February 19, 1988 Dr. Brian became chairman of UPI. When his parent company, Infotechnology Inc., filed for bankruptcy in 1991 taking UPI along with it, it was learned the folks at Infotechnology had been playing pretty fast and loose with UPI and its books. It seems while it was being reported UPI was doing well and taking in lots of money, the main client UPI was servicing was Infotechnology. Basically UPI was selling its service to itself and what money there was just kept going in circles. One was keeping the other afloat. Dr. Brian himself would end up in prison for his shady financial dealings involving UPI and FNN. His reputation for much of his adult life was suspect and if UPI staff had any objections to Vazquez-Rana and Rev. Moon, Dr. Brian should never have been let into the building.

The company was later purchased by the Middle East Broadcasting System which contained members of the Saudi Royal Family with European ties. This was done mainly to keep it out of the hands of what MEBS backers called Zionists who also wanted the UPI name. The brand name had a lot of equity and still does today. Of course what MEBS did was tragic in that it laid off everyone at the foreign bureaus and many US based bureaus leaving them without pensions.

MEBS eventually turned the company into a web based news service and then sold it to the Moonies anyway. Helen Thomas, long time UPI White House correspondent called it quits about this time. She had steadfastly stood on the statement she was never going to work for the Moonies anyway as did most of her colleagues when the wire service was still a wire service. By this time nearly all of the reporters and broadcasters had moved on. The drama of UPI unfolded over a long period of time and other jobs were in the offing for many.

The story of UPI fits here because it basically shows where and how the Internet rose to prominence in the journalistic field. UPI, a great icon of journalism, has been reduced to an Internet wire service employing freelance reporters around the globe. Many of whom could not come close to living up to the standards of those who came before them, let alone newspaper folks such as Woodward, Bernstein and Bradley. The UPI tradition was a proud one. Often UPI was second on a story to AP but the joke around the UPI newsroom was "AP got it first, UPI got it right."

Today a blogger, or the Internet reporter, is concerned about being first and only first. More hits will go to the website which breaks it first. Others will credit the website with breaking the story and give it legitimacy. It doesn't matter if the story is correct, nor has all the proper elements to back it up and show it is correct. It often doesn't matter even if the writing is bad or incorrect. Spell Check will take care of most of the grammar but this doesn't mean it is correct or even right, let alone done well.

With the death of paper newspapers, as opposed to on-line newspapers, comes the loss of legitimacy and with it the loss of jobs. Whereas small town local newspapers served a purpose, sold advertising and had large classified sections, today these cherished beacons of local news are gone or going fast. When was the last time you looked in a newspaper classified section for an apartment for rent or a home for sale? You don't do this anymore because it is simpler, easier and in many cases much better to go on-line to find that home or apartment. The good thing about the on-line shopper is you can get a virtual tour of the apartment or home before you take the next step to call. Of course what you are seeing is what the seller wants you to see and you have to physically go there anyway but the on-line tool for this is a major achievement.

It did not help the newspaper's bottom line because while the costs may be lower the income is definitely less. And if the newspaper doesn't offer the service for free someone else will. There we go with that word again; Free. You don't have to purchase the newspaper and there are lots of services offering the experience free to the seller. Why would someone do this? Hits to the website, customers to the website and the hope of selling adjacent advertising to the website. It is all about the Hits.

So now the advertising base is shrinking for newspapers because they can advertise for less money and better targeting with an on-line ad. The bloggers have replaced reporters and other on-line news services with video have also replaced the job reporters do for a newspaper. Photographers are needed and there work is being seen world wide but they are lucky to get paid for it because if someone else has the photo they will post it for FREE! The legitimate photographer sells his stuff to an on-line service if he can get them to buy it and it often appears all over the world without him seeing a dime because someone has lifted the photo. Just right click the mouse and click on "save image." The battle to stop this isn't working and has fallen on deaf ears.

So now reporters are out of jobs or are taking less pay, photographers are doing the same, and classified is dying and so is advertising. This brings about the end of the newspaper. The company which owns the newspaper will survive, maybe. If they work it out right they can continue as an on-line newspaper and if there is enough local people who want local content it will struggle along. It cannot compete with the general free services over the World Wide Web and never will be able to.

The Fifth Estate dies a hard death and major corporations with bottom line philosophies will buy up what there is. Who investigates them when they own all the newspapers and on-line services those investigative journalists used to work for? Does it get better? Aren't citizen journalists using their eyes and ears the best way to get the facts? Absolutely not. You will get more news by using citizen journalists but you won't get THE NEWS.

In November, 2010, a helicopter reporter for the CBS Television station in Los Angeles filmed, from a distance, a trail in the sky which looked exactly like a rocket being fired over the ocean. With several military bases nearby it only seemed natural. Calls were made but the military denied firing anything. The video was so convincing the story went viral. All over the world, hundreds of web sites, conspiracy theorists, anti-government bloggers and legitimate news sources grabbed the story.

The government was not only denying they fired anything into space but after a day they were denying it was a rocket. They talked about optical illusions and when the dust had cleared it seemed as if they were correct. The explanation, even to KNX News Radio investigative reporter Charles Feldman, himself a pilot, the explanation was legitimate. A contrail from a jetliner was the explanation. Feldman agreed with the government's explanation on the air while the host of the show didn't give it the same credence. In the end, the government stood by its decision and conspiracies abounded world wide. You can still see that video and the questions raised today on the Web.

Citizen journalists are being used more and more by legitimate news organizations and instead of airing calls on talk shows, emails are read. No exchanges or banter needed here. Citizen journalists are being urged to call in, report what they see and often give nothing more than opinion and even slanderous remarks on live radio and television. If a reporter who worked for the station said some of the things these citizen journalists are saying the legal department would have them fired or suspended on the spot.

They are even being encouraged to post photos of stories, fire coverage, police coverage and more to news agency web sites. Previously a paid photographer would be handling these jobs but today it is a citizen journalist doing it for free and a "whoopee my name and photo are on KW—TV" right now!

Jobs lost, work compromised and ethics out the window. This is the world of the Internet and this part of the world of journalism is not coming back. With corporations facing shareholders who want larger profits the cuts will keep coming. CBS for instance announced record profits during the final quarter of 2010. It was still asking for cuts and give backs in union negotiations during this time period from all of its labor unions. CBS was not alone. Banks were doing the same while holding on to record sums of cash during a time when small business could not get loans during the recession and more people were out of work than in the past 60 years. See the above section quoting former President Bill Clinton who points out the banks at this point in 2011 were sitting on $2 trillion in cash and not lending it.

It is not only newspapers but magazines which have been directly affected. Freelance reporters work much more cheaply than paid staffers and all publications have made good use of these freelance people for centuries. Today with the Internet however it is much worse and more difficult. With lower budgets with everything going on-line for free there is little use for freelancers because the editorial content has slipped. Magazines will print more advertising than they will journalistic column inches. Try picking up a mainstream magazine today and see how much editorial content there is between the Table of Contents and the first story. Chances are you will see half a dozen pages of advertisements before the first story. Much of the content will be masked in Survey's, Quizzes, E-Mail comment from readers and occasionally there will be some hard-core reporting. Not much of it will be there but there will be some.

Then there is the music industry.

Music on the Internet

The music business is no longer a real business as we knew it. There was a day when musicians made money in three ways. They wrote the music, they performed the music live or they recorded the music for distribution on records. At first they recorded it on wax, then slate and finally vinyl. CD's came along and with the dance mix craze singles eventually replaced albums to a point. Albums were still recorded and sold but with the advent of the cassette tape things went smaller and easier to handle. This was after the bulky eight-track phase.

Soon the CD was everywhere from your home to your car and before long on a hand held device. Tapes were gone, CD's raged and then the DVD came along so you could watch your favorite band perform as well as listen to them. Then this was replaced by digital music. Musicians actually loved this because their concerts were preserved forever and they could be sold. Things moved along pretty well but the video soon became more important than the music itself. Songs were created specifically for the video ride. The music didn't matter as it was just something to add to the video for a three minute film of the artist. MTV started the craze and eventually had to branch out as well.

At one point musicians, tired of being robbed of their royalties by unscrupulous managers, agents and record producers chose to only record music they wrote and registered. The songwriter was now the song performer in nearly all cases and they collected the bulk of the royalties from the music. The record companies for decades had their way with new acts who despite being talented were not very money wise. They wanted to become hit makers and millionaires at the same time. The former was usually all they got while the record companies took care of the latter.

So by now musicians were making lots of money writing, performing, sometimes producing and even distributing their music. They could make money many different ways as long as the music sold. Then came the Internet and it all changed forever.

In the late 1990's Shawn Fanning, a student at Northeastern came up with a way to share MP3 music files which eventually led to the company named Napster. Napster eventually also became synonymous with music theft, copyright infringement and the beginning of the ruination of the music business model as we knew it.

Basically Napster stored millions of pieces of music which were then shared by its up to 26 million users at no charge. Instead of buying a CD for $15 and the artist getting his fair share, consumers could just download the music from Napster, put it on their own CD produce a bootleg copy and listen whenever they wanted for free. Users who purchased the music in a previous format such as cassette tape or CD felt justified in downloading the music since they "had already paid for it once."

They also shared it with others who also created their own CD's. In theory Napster could buy just one CD of a new album from a group such as Metallica, put it on-line and those who downloaded it could share it with anyone who wanted it and a second CD might never be sold. Thus who gets cheated but Metallica? It was by the way Metallica which brought a copyright infringement against Napster and eventually won its case. NAPSTER went bankrupt and sold off its assets.

It did not matter anymore because the damage had been done. Now people who bought the CD would just share it with whomever they wanted on the Internet and the entire system cheated artists out of millions of dollars in royalties. It became very hard to stop and was even more difficult than halting the Chinese from producing $1 DVD's of new films. These are commonly sold to tourists on the streets of Beijing right in the open as police just walk by.

Through a system of legal wrangling between record companies and artists a pay for download system was finally developed to legally allow people to download music. The artist still made some money but not nearly as much. The Napster fiasco did allow new musicians to get their music heard and today whenever a group or musician wants to break his record out onto the public they usually debut it on the Internet. The Internet has become a useful promotional tool but at the expense of millions of dollars being taken right out of the hands of the creators of the same music.

"When it came to Intellectual Property rights the music industry was paramount in trying to enact antipiracy laws, and the first stage was to limit downloading which finally closed the door on Napster," said Dr. Pamela Falk.

Dr. Falk teaches United Nations studies and International Economics at Hunter College in New York. She is also a Resident Correspondent at the United Nations.

"Artists were not getting paid royalties for all their work. It wasn't fair not to give royalties to Roberta Flack and Lady Gaga when they have worked so hard at creating their music," she said. "They make their money in royalties and the record industry took the lead and closed Napster, and it is the same with movies. There were dozens of sites that, for free, enabled people to share their music and movies. But writing legislation which limited large internet sites like Google and Wikipedia was a problem because understandably they felt they should not be held responsible for all that goes up on their platform."

Someone will always find a way to get around the law and the Internet, being in its infancy, is full of loopholes.

One argument is when technology changes things you just have to adapt. Others would argue why should the creator adapt when technology just makes it easer to break the law by stealing?

"The industries which rely on royalties are going to have to adapt," Falk added. "If royalties are not part of the equation going forward then the industries involved have to figure out how to make money for artists."

The music and entertainment business are very difficult places to make a living. When you consider an actor goes on 90-100 auditions and may get one job – meaning they get turned down 99 times – egos become fragile and the job of waiting tables ends up paying the bills. It was always difficult and despite the rewards given to those who made it big, or even semi-big, less than five percent of all the actors in Hollywood make a living just acting. It is similar in the music business. This is why musicians began only performing the music they wrote so they could actually make a living. With the introduction of the Internet they began asking what gives people the right to steal our music without ever paying a dime for it. They were correct and the courts sided with them. Neither they nor the courts could fight the overwhelming power of the Internet though and people just ignored the law because they could get the music for free. There is that word again.

Eventually with the development of new laws, people who felt downloading off the Internet really was stealing were able to purchase the music for about 99-cents a download in most case. Not much but if an artist made a few pennies off a million downloads it was something.

The record companies continued to push the idea they were losing millions of dollars in sales. The Internet is a great place to promote new ideas but it definitely inhibits profit margins despite the fact more sales may be made in the long run.

In 2011 Georgia Music Partners (GMP), a non-profit organization, did a study on the music industry in the southern state. The study, conducted by Dr. B. William Riall Ph.D. estimated the music industry's economic impact on Georgia alone was $3.7 billion a year. The study also credited the industry with creating nearly 20,000 jobs and bringing in $313 million in taxes to state and local coffers. These amounts were in the Internet age. Imagine the numbers if those jobs lost were still being filled.

Many file sharing networks exist in the post agreement age but the biggest is Apple's iTunes. iTunes remains the place where you can go to buy and download music for a small price. It hasn't stopped people from stealing it and putting it up on the social networking site YouTube. Occasionally YouTube removes a song tied to a video when someone objects. Millions of pieces of music remain on the site however too many to police because anyone can place anything on YouTube for free. Some of these videos with their music have been viewed and listened to hundreds of thousands of times.

For instance, a person by the name of Joseph Fulton posted the most highly viewed video as of Thanksgiving 2010 of Gordon Lightfoot's *"The Wreck of the Edmund Fitzgerald"* on YouTube with a home made video to highlight the story and the music. It is one of dozens of such videos using this song to the photos and pictures of the story of the shipwreck which took 29 lives in the 1970's on Lake Superior. As of the time we checked for this book (November 2010) there were 871,669 views of the video. Now that video has been tagged by YouTube with the statement; "the audio has been removed from this video." This was followed by instructions to see it with the audio at another spot via a link. So in other words YouTube had seen the light and realized this was copyright infringement and removed the audio only to redirect viewers to the spot where they could see and hear the video.

The other videos using this bootlegged music were also seen hundreds of thousands of times, some with audio removed others with audio intact. Undoubtedly a few people, based on their experience in watching the video, did go out and purchase a Gordon Lightfoot CD. How much did Lightfoot lose from the several million others who did not and got it for free? Many certainly downloaded the music for free from the video.

News organizations illegally do this all the time. They need a clip of music to go with a news story about a singer or an event so they go right to YouTube and download the sound from the video. It was already stolen so they just used the stolen music one more time. Much of the time it is even used without credit let alone without payment. Radio stations may have a blanket agreement enabling them to use these songs legally just as they play music on the air, however.

If you ask any musician, especially those who also sell their CD's and DVD's at their concerts and performances, they would rather be back in the days before the Internet when it came to making a living. This will never happen. The Internet is free and someone will always come along to make a cheaper mousetrap and put it on the Internet. CD's are cheap to make and reproduce. The promotional aspects behind them are not.

Take for instance a record company and what it did for the business. How many people previously were employed before the

Internet? There were limo drivers who drove the artists, packaging people, artists to develop the print products, promotional people, salesmen, and all of their support staff. This portion of the industry has shrunk because the Internet has taken over much of the overhead and certainly much of the profit used to hire and pay these people.

The business model which was the standard before the Internet is no longer. You must compete in the Internet world of slim profits and this isn't going to change. The reason is, there is no cost involved in stealing the music and very little if you buy it from a place such as iTunes. There is a very slim profit margin if any and there is no real barrier to entry.

General Business on the Internet

You might be asking yourself at this point "So what does this Internet business thing have to do with me?" The real answer is "Everything." There is not one business in the world today not affected in some way, shape or form by the Internet. Let us take a look at 10 of the businesses we have not discussed previously in this book and look at the ways in which they are adversely or even positively affected by on-line sales and traffic.

The first one we will look at is one which you might not see as having anything to do with the Internet. The local grocery store is a place you and I go at least once a week and maybe more depending on our lifestyle and family situation. We drive up and get out of our cars, walk inside, grab a basket and start our weekly chore of walking up and down the aisles looking for what we need and what fits our fancy. If you are like me you might get hooked on a smell of a certain food as you walk down the aisle. Whether we need that food or not, it sort of just jumps right into our basket. The cinnamon rolls that look so tasty on the package and smell so good as we walk by the store bakery just wander into the basket we are wheeling and if they make it to the counter we take them home.

So is this store affected by the Internet? Look at the company website. For instance, if you go to Vons website for one of the larger grocery store chains on the West Coast you will see everything you can get in the store by walking in, you can get on-line delivered right to your door. At the time we looked you also got 10-percent off your first purchase and FREE Delivery! There is that word again; Free.

How about a complete Thanksgiving Day Dinner hot and prepared delivered to your door for $39.99? Try this once and chances are you will never go shopping again for all the fixin's for T-Day. You can even join the company on-line club for additional savings. Sounds like a great idea for the elderly who may not be able to get out as much as before and have problems teetering through the aisle with a shopping cart. This is a wonderful innovation. It also might come in handy for the very busy executive who lives alone.

On many of the grocery store websites you will find if you buy on-line you may not only get Free Delivery but the items may be cheaper than if you walked into the store for specific items. This might be the age old "come on" we've heard so much about. The same as in the car business they put an item out there for you to buy, you do and you get hooked on doing it the easy way; point and click. You will never have to go to the grocery store again.

Sounds nice and easy. If you never went to the grocery store again and everyone else followed suit – which is totally feasible in the next 20 to 30 years as kids who grow up this way become adults who know of no other way to shop – there would be no need for check out clerks, box boys and box girls, in-store sample givers who promote the products, or employees to stock the shelves. There would only be a need for warehouse people to box up the items. UPS and Fed Ex and now even the United States Postal Service will pick up the packages from the warehouse and deliver them. What about the company which cleans the parking lot? No need for them anymore because you don't have a public parking lot because the store front itself no longer exists. Each store of medium size would likely lose at least 25 jobs meaning 25 more people would be out of work and won't be able to afford those groceries anymore anyway.

Fresh and Easy is a neighborhood grocery store chain run by a British company in the United States. They have already done away with check out clerks and like many other chains are offering discounts if you bring your own bags to bag your own groceries. They even sell re-usable cloth grocery bags. Good for the environment, good for business in the short run.

A second business affected by the Internet you might not really expect to be affected is insurance. Before 2005 had you ever really heard of Progressive, Geico, The General, E-surance or were you just familiar with Farmers, State Farm, Travelers and 21st Century? Today you can go right on-line and compare prices for insurance with any number of companies, major or minor. With the click of a mouse you can find out if you will be paying $356 a month to insure your 1998 Corvette or $375 with another company. The commercials you see on television are fairly accurate as to how fast you will know what you will be paying and if you want the add-ons to raise the price.

It is like the old joke of the man who went into a Chinese restaurant and ordered one from Column A and two from Column B. You pick what you want, add them up and there you have it.

This menu of services has brought to the forefront any number of smaller companies whom you never heard of before to compete with the big companies. Dueling insurance firms have had to adjust their policies (no pun intended) to compete with the fledgling insurers. State Farm may be bigger than Company A but Company A is offering you the same coverage for 20-percent less. How can they do this? They have less overhead because they have no agents, no offices, no expense accounts and virtually very few people. In other words it is mostly done on the Internet where there is very little Barrier to Entry.

It was just a few years ago 20th Century Insurance (now 21st and formerly a part of AIG) advertised it had lower rates because it did not have any insurance salesmen. This worked and 20th Century became a major insurance company in the western United States. It kept the costs down and legitimately passed on those costs to the consumer. It insured only drivers at the time.

However, 20th Century had very strict rules. Not anyone would qualify for insurance with 20th Century. If you did you got the lowest rates possible, very good coverage and you stayed with them for life. If you did have a few accidents they would not renew your policy and as one driver found out the following scenario fell into place.

"You were paying $550 a year with 20th Century but your rate with us at the Auto Club is going to be $750," the AAA salesmen told Richard B.

"Why so much?" Richard B., asked.

"Well, sir, you were with 20th Century which is the lowest when it comes to rates," answered the salesman. "Now you have to enter the other world of insurers."

Basically, 20th Century worked as long as the rest of the insurance companies did not follow suit. Enter the Internet where lots of insurers have followed in the footsteps of 20th Century. The company also spread out and insures more than just cars and trucks. Home owners were added to the mix as well at one point.

The Internet has spawned a whole slew of budget insurance firms where the only real non-insurance cost to the company is advertising.

Geico with its talking Gecko, the Cavemen, and celebrities doing odd things put a major dent in the competition. Some of the most creative and memorable television commercials ever produced were for this insurer. Progressive had a very nice run with Flo, the young lady who was the company television commercial spokeswoman. More people knew Flo than ever knew their insurance agent when they had one.

The major companies had to move to the on-line arena and while still doing business out of neighborhood storefronts these insurance brokers were finding it more difficult to meet with people than ever before. In 2010 someone who was over 50 years old would still seek out a friendly face to walk into an office and chat with them about their insurance needs. Someone who was between 40 and 50 would likely go into the same insurance office armed with information from the Internet and their mailbox. The under 40 crowd wouldn't bother. They'd shop on-line and set up payments direct from their bank account or credit card. Their children would never even know what an insurance salesman was.

Take for instance a field we have long since seen as historical. My father passed away in 1983. For over 50 years he worked as a *home delivery milkman*. Some of you reading this have never heard the term. Up until about 1965 many Americans still got their milk delivered to their door by a man dressed in a uniform who might even have a key to your home. He usually got up at 3:00 in the morning, loaded his truck at the dairy and set about on his rounds at 5:00 in the morning delivering milk.

My father, like so many others, would visit your home three days a week on average. There was usually a metal box or a tray on your porch (depending on what part of the country you lived in, cold or warm weather) and inside would be empty bottles he would take and replace them with fresh bottles of milk. Later on wax cartons replaced the bottles. These cartons were lighter, cheaper and could easily be disposed of in the trash.

If you preferred to have your milk placed directly into your refrigerator my father had a key to open the door, usually the kitchen door, and he'd put the milk in the fridge and if there were empties he'd take those as well. He also delivered eggs, cheese, butter and during the holidays cookies and candy. It was a great service. It was a service which cost extra.

Around 1966 supermarkets began selling milk much more cheaply than the milkman could deliver it. Drive through dairies opened up, usually by the same dairy the driver worked for, so people could buy the same things directly from the dairy and cut out the middle man – my father. Combine the drive-in dairy (now almost non-existent) with the supermarket price (people figured they had to go to the store to grocery shop anyway) and soon the milkman was out of business. In a handful of cities a similar service still exists for the rich mainly but just like the insurance salesman of the early 2000's the milkman is no longer a part of American society.

Ask a 20-something if they know what a *home delivery milkman* is and they won't have a clue. An entire workforce was done away with due to short sightedness and profit motives. At least to the markets and the dairy there was a cost to entry. They had to build places to sell milk and the American public at the time chose convenience over service. With the insurance salesperson and the explosion of on-line insurers it is not the same. It is basically for the same reason as so many other businesses; no barrier to entry.

A third industry affected tremendously by the Internet is the movie business. The rise in technology drove the industry to new heights in the 1990's and put actors in jeopardy. They would still do voice work but the need for actors was dwindling. With the technological advances for animating movies there has become less of a need for real bodies to act and in a field where less than 5-percent of the work force are "working actors" making a living at their craft, this was a deadly blow.

By 2010 when *Avatar* came out the industry had advanced to the point where it seemed the vast majority of the films making a profit were techno films. The new animation had replaced actors except for voice work and this was even changing. Using computers voices can be created not only re-created.

Enter the Internet and the low cost of distribution. In previous years films went to the Festival scene (mainly Cannes) and deals were made to pick up these movies for distribution. They were eventually run into theaters around the United States before moving into the international theater scene. A film might be in US movie houses for weeks before going international. The Internet changed much of that and mainly because on occasion films were being shown on-line before they hit theaters in the United States. Such distribution was usually illegal but once it was out there it couldn't be stopped. One person with a bootlegged copy of a film which had not been released could distribute it to millions of people in a matter of hours.

How many people would pay the $10 to see a film they could get for free on the Internet or they could purchase via bootlegged DVD for a couple of bucks? The vast number of people who would pay for the theater experience was dwindling due to home video, on-line video and rising costs. The production value of home theater was also rising in quality. By 2011 the average cost of a ticket to see a new film at the theater had risen to about $15 and sometimes more. The reason the price of tickets went up was because fewer people were going out to see films when they could either wait a short while for the DVD or, as was the new trend, they could see it on-line for free. Eventually producers moved to put their film on-line before it hit the theater. There was a small charge but those who *had* to see the film early could watch it on their television or computer even though they did pay for it.

The visual effects of a bootlegged copy were not overwhelming at first but this soon began to change. With it was the fortunes of the studios as more independent films (or Indies) were being made at a lower cost. Actors were taking anything to come their way just to work. The words "back end" became common. Actors and even directors and producers would work for free on a film project with a promise if the film actually made money they would get paid on "the back end," or well after the film had run its course.

With Internet theft and films being distributed on-line, studios and producers were struggling to make films which would bring in crowds at the box office. Making movies became even more risky than it had ever been and it was always a risk judging what the public wanted to see. Producers and studios were very careful to pick and choose and fewer and fewer films were "green lighted" and made. Profits fell and actors found it even tougher to find work – or at least work which paid when they did the job.

The reason so many remakes of older hit films became popular is they had a built-in audience of about 60-percent according to industry surveys. There was little risk in making a film which had already been proven a hit 50 years ago. There was a built-in older audience plus a new audience. It was a formula for success.

In their 2006 study Professors Amit Joshi (University of Central Florida) and Dominique Hanssens (UCLA and Marketing Science Institute) pointed out the numbers game is the biggest part of the equation. It is the reason studios are not making films like they previously did.

"Major studios typically launch fewer than 20 motion pictures per year," the study on Movie Advertising and the Stock Market Valuation of Studios states. "So the financial performance of a single movie release can have a major effect on the studio's profitability."

In their study the two professors concluded advertising was a huge and maybe the biggest factor in determining whether the studio made money overall. They discovered too much advertising after the film was released, actually affected the stock market price of the studio negatively rather than positively. The simple reason was a huge amount of post launch advertising brought too high of an expectation regarding the film's performance. If the film did well, this was expected. If the over hyped film did not do well the studio suffered.

"Our findings also suggest that movies that are hits at the box office, may result in the lowering of the stock price if they had high media support on account of high expectations build-up prior to launch."

Dollars taken in for movies were up in 2009 and the trend was mainly based on higher ticket prices. The Motion Picture Association of America (MPAA) reported sales in 2009 at just under $30 billion. In North America ticket sales were actually down by about 1.7 million, or down to 1.4 billion tickets sold.

Movie studios were also taking fewer risks by offering more to actors, directors and writers on the "back end" rather than paying them for their work directly. The back end meant if the picture did well the artists would get paid more but if it didn't they shared the risk.

The end result was actors, for instance, became more choosy when it came to selecting roles to play. No one wants to work for free and if the film didn't get picked up by a big distributor or just plain didn't do well they may just end up doing exactly that; working for free.

The Internet was making it much easier to make a movie and put it out there for everyone to see on-line. Making money on the film was another story. Making films is art and in nearly every case also business. If a film has no return on investment there won't be a second film for the artists. Studios are still making money due to prudent choices and fewer of them along with higher prices and making sure distribution includes the Internet with some sort of return on investment no matter how little it is.

Television fell into the same mold but in this case producers took advantage of the on-line arena to make money without paying what they normally would pay actors. Actors traditionally got longer term payments. In most cases they got paid for their work when the television show ran a second or third time on some secondary network. These were called "residuals." Actors counted on them for future pay. An actor might perform in one successful series in his lifetime. The residuals could keep coming for years allowing the actor to continue to pursue a career in acting.

When the Internet came along the producers would re-sell the shows and entire series to on-line companies to show for free on the Internet. The on-line company might make money from the adjacent advertising which increased when more people went to their website to watch these shows for free. The increased "hits" made the site more desirable to advertisers who would have to pay a lot less to advertise on the website than they ever did for television.

The actors got nothing for this "new media." Since the producers owned the shows and the contracts were signed before the new forms of media were developed (i.e. the Internet and in some cases DVD sales as well as Text and cell phone video) they didn't have to pay the actors as they would if the shows ran on independent television stations. The Internet had replaced an entire class of distribution and it did it basically for Free. There is that word again; Free.

The future for actors was up in the air with all of this. Soon New Media became the focus of every union negotiation regarding performing. If you could watch an entire movie on your cell phone where would it all end? No one knew and everyone conjectured. It became a nightmare for performers who could see their livelihood disappearing right before their eyes.

Not to be outdone newscasters and reporters in the radio field were facing the same dilemma. Radio reporters from several companies were being told they had to carry cameras with them in the field. With the emergence of station fed websites on the Internet radio reporters were being told they had to contribute to the content for the website as part of their job. This of course did not sit well with the reporters because the company was now asking them to do this for no extra pay. They were also asked to carry video cameras which were light weight and handheld. Again no extra pay was to be had for this extra work.

They were being asked to do additional work for free because it was going on the Internet and at the time websites were not usually making money, any money. They were image builders for the stations and if there was advertising it was a bonus because it didn't take much capital to keep a website on-line and running. That is especially true if the content being provided is free. In addition it was going to take jobs away from legitimate camera people who worked for the same company's TV station. Radio was now feeding TV thus eliminating the need for TV cameramen or at least reducing their role.

Radio reporters could see their jobs being jeopardized as did disc jockeys who were already being moved out with bigger network fed shows. The puzzling thing about the new Internet radio was commercial radio was FREE already which is one of the beauties of commercial radio stations. However, with the advent of the Internet new radio programs were springing up all over the world offering a wide variety of formats from long form interview shows to Christian music stations. Anyone could have his or her own radio show at virtually no cost. You could start your own radio station on the Internet for Free. Oh, must I say it again, there is that word; Free.

Most of the people who ran Internet radio didn't really care to make a living at it. It was more of a personal desire to do it. Sure everyone wants to be a star but these people just really wanted a voice for the most part. They were not making any money at it. I was interviewed for several of these shows on the Internet when my first book came out "Fan Letters to a Stripper; A Patti Waggin Tale." The title and the genre; burlesque, intrigued a number of them and we did anywhere from 20 minutes to a half hour interview. Easy for Internet or virtual radio, very rare for commercial or what came to be known as terrestrial radio.

How many folks actually heard these shows I will never know. Some of these interviewers produced newsletters for their listeners on their websites and had developed email lists. They also may be selling products through their newsletters or blogs. Only they could tell you how many listeners they have because the nice thing about Internet radio is you get an hourly readout and much more detailing who and when and how long people listen to something on your website. Another cottage industry developed these programs but it employs very few people per company.

So from movies to radio the Internet has had this job changing, if not job costing affect. It has replaced legitimate well trained workers with non-trained individuals who virtually work for free or not much more than free.

A fourth business affected in a negative way by the Internet has almost disappeared because of the Internet. When was the last time you went to a travel agent to book a vacation? At best they have adapted to an Internet model doing exactly what you can do for yourself. At worst they have closed up shop and are looking for a job.

Before the Internet you basically had three choices when planning a vacation. For airfares and cruises you could call or write the airlines or cruise lines directly. The endless time sitting on hold during the main part of the day while you were calling on your lunch break has not been missed.

You could map out a road trip making sure to stop to visit relatives along the way hoping they would offer you a free night's stay and a couple of free meals. Often you would drive a hundred miles out of your way to visit a distant relative you barely knew and didn't particularly like in hopes of saving the cost of a hotel room only to find out they offered you the local Motel Six instead.

Then there was the travel agent. She or he was the friendly face behind a desk with a rack of brochures on the wall to exotic places such as Egypt and Spain. They would help you plan out your vacation and take a percentage of the total bill for doing so. They had the connections and all the answers and could even give you those little tips about where to go and when because they likely had been there themselves half a dozen times. The travel agent usually took a few days to work out the details within your budget and a few more weeks to get all the documents into your hands. It cost you more certainly but everything was done for you and in retrospect you didn't mind the agent making a living on the commissions taken from the airlines, the cruise lines, the hotels and the theme parks so you could get away for a couple of weeks.

Today everything the agent did for you can be done *by* you on the Internet. It is not only more efficient and much faster but you could work out the many different scenarios from your home computer and come up with different options and pricing. For instance, you are going to Italy and you have been there enough to know you really want to avoid Rome, Florence and Naples. Instead you want to stay in Grieve, Odolo and Potenza. A travel agent may not have had those at her fingertips for you and it might take weeks to follow up and make such arrangements. Small hotels in those towns would likely only take faxes and the time and cost would be prohibitive.

Today, on the Internet you can book small villas in all of those places in a matter of hours, work out the driving details, train schedules and meals all from your home. You can even purchase much of it via credit card the same way. The end result is a much cheaper, more personal vacation and thousands of travel agents who are now looking for work. Like the home delivery milkman discussed previously it is a service industry which has run its course. The travel agent industry however was directly related to the Internet which offers the same service an agent did but for Free. Oh my gosh there it is again; Free. The bummer is you don't have that friendly face just a phone call away to ask about anything you might have a question about.

Number five industry is the pornography industry. Depending on your point of view and possible moral and religious beliefs the Internet may be just what the doctor ordered. Yes the Internet has helped kill the home porn market of DVD's and magazines but porn is the fastest growing industry on the Internet. Why is this so? Simply because it is cheaper.

The entire MILF (Moms I'd Like to F—k) genre was started by two horny young men with a handheld video camera and a lot of balls. The idea was to approach horny 30-50 year old housewives whose partners were not as interested in sex as they were in their younger days and to offer these women the opportunity to have sex with two young studs on camera for a small fee. It worked and then turned itself into a two headed monster. Soon real porn stars were starring in mock MILF video's moving away from the original business plan. Well the real business plan was to get these two young entrepreneurs laid as often as possible but this is beside the point.

Since we are talking about the real world of business the porn industry and the Internet cannot be ignored. The industry itself has been around for thousands of years depending on the media available. First it was cave art, followed by drawings on paper and paint on canvas. When photography came about it grew even to a wider degree. Motion pictures added action to sex and the "Blue Movie" was created. Massage parlors and houses of prostitution were just a part of the industry.

When Video Tape reared its ugly head, porn moved from the Pussy Cat Theatre in the seedy section of town, to your own living and bed rooms. The advent of CDs and DVDs made porn easier to sell and easier to copy. Pornography and the sex tape era so to speak were still booming. Sex sells at every level and with the push for safe sex due to the AIDs epidemic and STDs what could be more safe than a sex DVD and your own hands. Even if you had a partner with the more liberal standards being practiced in the early 2000's women were as apt to rent a porn DVD as were men. Certain taboo situations were becoming more acceptable to every day Americans. Girl-girl sex was the rage and was even being exploited on television with several Gay and Lesbian TV networks coming about. And more women were having sex with women so the industry was growing due to the variety being offered.

Then the Internet joined the pleasures of sex and while the sex didn't increase the industry did. Sex exploded on the Internet and often in the most horrible ways. Not only was the free download a standard in the industry but the voyeurism and the chat rooms were springing up all over. Anyone with a mini-cam and a free website could be a porn star and there were no shortages of those who wanted to be the same. Girls and guys would walk through their homes on live video 24 hours a day. You could watch them sleeping, peeing, having sex, eating, cooking or any number of mundane things. Someone got the idea you could charge for this privilege. You could and the first folks in made some money.

Then someone offered the same service cheaper and cheaper and eventually there were free sites. The regular porn sites were offering free clips of a couple minutes long or just enough to wet your appetite before you rolled out your credit card number and bought a full download. Soon the free clips were getting longer and there were more of them so you really didn't need a full download to do what you needed to do. You got what you previously got at the Pussy Cat Theatre for Free!

It certainly cut into sales of DVDs which while they were not that expensive to make the cost of adult film actresses was. Box covers and photo shoots were perhaps more costly than making the film itself but there were costs, there were lots of lawyers to pay and there were shrinking profit margins due to the Internet.

And while some might rejoice at this, remember, the sex industry wasn't shrinking, it was growing and it was growing to the point where everyone and anyone had access because it was free on the Internet. And there are few controls on the Internet whereas the porn industry itself found itself continually boxed in and fighting legal battles in local municipalities. They were governed there but not so much on the Internet.

In addition, the Internet became a safe haven for child pornography and crimes against children. Stories abound where young girls were lured by lying old men who gave them a line behind a faceless Internet chat ID only to end up being raped or even worse. The Internet has been the place where pedophiles exchange volumes of photos and connections to small boys and girls who turn up missing each year. And perhaps the reason is because there is no cost to doing this kind of business on the Internet. It is free.

The sixth industry to receive more nails in its coffin is the DVD and Video Rental Stores. Tower Records and Blockbuster being the two big ones heading down the tubes in recent years. Before them went the small independent stores which also sold everything from knick-knacks to baseball cards and soda. They really did well by making their stores movie experience friendly for a while. They sold easy to pop popcorn; larger candy bars such as you would buy in a movie theater and lots of other things to make your "home movie night" a good experience.

When the DVD replaced the VHS tape these stores took a hit because they were being stuck with inventory and they had to replace every title in the store with a new medium. This was costly but not insurmountable and was the cost of doing business. The Internet could not be overcome.

When the Internet debuted it was only a matter of time before download technology grew so fast streaming was something anyone could do from a home PC or Mac. Whether it was bootlegged or available legitimately it was there to download in seconds to your home computer and then uploaded onto a DVD. All of this was costing less than $1 to accomplish. And you could make copies for your friends or just send them an email attachment and let them make their own DVD.

No longer would you need to rent a video, return it on time or pay a penalty and no longer would millions of people who worked at these stores have jobs. The way of Blockbuster was the way of the past and it was not coming back. There was also no replacement for it which would bring new jobs to the forefront.

Industry no. 7 has to be the retail book industry. It is virtually dead although the major chains are adapting. Mom and pop book store owners will soon no longer exist. There are basically two types of book stores under the old business model.

First, there is the local book store which sells new books but may also sell some used books. The store would likely also sell some other items such as posters, baseball cards and magazines.

There is also the chain store version of this such as Borders (which could not compete and folded in 2011) and Barnes & Noble. These chain stores target new book buyers but also sell magazines and usually have a Starbucks or some other kind of coffee house inside the store where people can sit, chat, work and enjoy while they also often read. It is a nice touch.

The other type of book store is the "Rare Book Store." This is a store usually tucked away in a corner of some side street and is run by someone who has either done it all their professional lives or by a retired person who really is living on a pension and doesn't need the money. These stores deal in expensive and not so expensive but hard to find books. They may have a safe where they keep the rarest of books which might be a First Edition of a book printed in the 1700's by a famous author and which retails for maybe $5,000. These book stores cater to a very exclusive clientele which often never comes into the store to shop. The owner keeps tabs on his exclusive clients and calls them if a book they would like comes in.

The Internet has affected both kinds of stores in a major way. In the case of the latter, the rare book seller, these stores have pretty much dried up around the country if not around the world simply because of the Internet. There really isn't a need to have such a shop because the seller can do almost all of his work from the confines of his office at home. Instead of paying for a retail space he simply sells to his clients on the Internet. The website he has for basically very little cost provides everything he needs. That is except one thing – a place to buy from.

One of the key elements, if not the main element to owning such a store is it offers sellers a handy place to sell their merchandise and the buyer/seller a way to continually restock his merchandise. Sitting at home in an office offers little opportunity to buy and replenish and to get those deals which for centuries have walked in the door. Yes you can find those deals on the Internet where there is great competition from others in the same industry as well as the same clients you want to sell your wares to. The Internet has basically destroyed this part of many businesses, especially collectibles.

The clients of the rare book seller of course don't need him anymore. They can now search the Web themselves for that rare book and usually pick it up cheaper than the middle man was willing to sell it for.

As the Internet grew in prominence in the sports and memorabilia world many of us who had retail stores only kept them open to buy. Believe it or not almost every day we were open someone walked in with something to sell. Most of it we rejected as not worth our time or money but a very good portion we did buy and resold for a very nice profit. It is the way these industries work. In our case what finally shut our doors was the 2008 recession and stock market crash. If not for that we might still have that retail location and might still be buying. On an average basis we pumped over $50,000 a year back into the local community purchasing goods from customers who then used that money to do everything from pay bills to buying groceries. And we had a very small location in a small town. Imagine the buying power of other such stores who spent hundreds of thousands of dollars a year back into the community.

The rare book seller will always have a home but as time passes and the Internet drives them out of business it is not the kind of industry which replenishes itself with knowledgeable people. As these dinosaurs die off, finding younger versions to replace them and open such stores becomes almost impossible.

The retail book seller has been affected in quite a different way but still adversely affected. The Internet has provided competition of unbelievable proportions and has literally killed off wide segments of the industry. Amazon has done its best to drive local retail stores of all kinds out of their own industries by offering millions of items for pennies over cost in order to make sales.

Since we are talking particularly about books in this chapter we'll confine our words to just books at this point. Let us take one book in particular. I won't use the name because the author is a friend of mine and I don't want to encourage price cutting of his book. Let us call his book "Dragonfly." Dragonfly was a mid-expensive art book, hard bound and full of great artwork. It carried a Suggested Retail Price of $49.99. If you looked inside the cover the price was $49.99. Books usually sell at some sort of discount except at smaller stores which buy them from a distributor at slightly over cost, say 10-percent and they have to pay for shipping in many cases.

This particular book could be purchased in 40 book lots for $28 or roughly 55-percent of the Suggested Retail Price (SRP). If the store or the distributor bought 20 of the books they would get it for a little bit more or $30. If the store bought just a handful they would pay about $35 per book or about the same perhaps from their distributor. It is an expensive book and won't sell like hotcakes unless you are an art store with a large clientele. So most local book stores will probably buy them at $35 and resell them for $49.99 or perhaps $45 to good customers or discount them for the holidays.

The book price debuted on Amazon at $36 and was eligible for free shipping. Other booksellers on line were less than $40 as well. In Europe and other countries it was selling for more than the SRP but here in the USA it was selling at barely above cost. A year after release Amazon had sellers from $22 to $36 while several other on-line sellers had the book listed for $29.99.

Out of the gate how could anyone expect the local book store to compete with an on-line price of $1.00 over what they themselves had paid for it and only a few dollars more than the lowest, direct from the publisher cost. The advantage of throwing in free shipping, which is about $5, is enough to drive the mom and pop retailer out of business. It has in many cases.

It doesn't stop there. Put every book in the store into this same scenario with most books carrying a price tag of $10-$25.

Even paperbacks fall into the same fate and they sell for less than $10.

Here are some new release examples showing the same kind of problem befalling the book industry. The week it was released "Decision Points" by former President George W. Bush was reduced by Amazon from the list price of $35 to $18.77. This is 46-percent off the cover price. The same week "Diary of a Wimpy Kid: The Ugly Truth" debuted with a SRP of $13.96. Amazon had it the day of release for $6.94! This is half the suggested retail price. The very next week "Unbroken: A World War Two Story of Survival, Resilience, and Redemption" sold for $27 if you looked at the list price. Amazon offered it the day it hit store shelves for $13.99.

If you think these are just odd titles think again. The same was being done during the same weeks for new books by Stephen King, John Grisham, Barbra Streisand and Glenn Beck. Hundreds of books offered at half the price, barely over cost and at prices well below what local book stores were paying let alone selling.

The major chain stores were also trying to compete by offering great deals on line and the competition became even fiercer. Eventually, the thought of even opening a book store in a local town was out of the question. The Internet had destroyed these businesses and put thousands if not millions of people out of work. Even more so was the damage it did to the industry and the public as well. With libraries closing due to budget cuts where was someone who loved to read going to go to browse and learn? The local bookstore was quickly fading from the scene.

Perhaps the largest group of businesses to be threatened if not destroyed by the Internet was retail itself. By the year 2008 the line between retail and wholesale had been obliterated. It no longer existed in most businesses. The business model was ripped through like a runaway train and it wasn't coming back. Once consumers saw they could purchase a widget for ten cents instead of 15 cents they would never go back to buy another widget for 15 cents again. In fact, they would probably try to buy it for 8-cents.

The problem is when consumers buy from someone who barely makes a profit on the item the seller will eventually re-evaluate their situation and the re-evaluation won't be to raise prices. It will be to cut costs as has been the legend which we live by. Where are the first cuts going to be made? Workers and jobs are the most expensive and visible part of the business.

"We can do it with less," the bosses decry. "Cut the work force by 10-percent which is what we hate to do but it is what we have to do."

Those laid off workers now have no money to spend. Those who do have jobs continue to buy at the bargain prices, in turn leading to fewer profits for the companies where they spend their money (grocery, clothing etc.). These companies in turn lay off more workers. They may be the same workers who paid 8 to 10 cents for those widgets. Now they can't even afford to buy widgets at any price. This affects the first company even more.

The company finally can't sell enough widgets to keep the business open and shuts down, laying off the rest of the workers it employed. It is a scenario we've seen over and over again. It happened long before the Internet but since the Internet it is happening at a more rapid pace in many fields.

Look around your town and see how many businesses are now vacant shops and stores. The new firms which are springing up via the eternal optimists are businesses which provide a service to the consumer not a product. They are not damaged as much by the Internet because the individual provides a service which must be done directly by the business owners.

There are massage parlors, tattoo parlors, repair shops, mortgage brokers which are somewhat affected by the Internet, coffee shops, pizza places, plumbers and any manner of service oriented business. You don't see very many retail stores springing up selling products either which are needed or desired. The widget sellers are not looking for new business locations but are rather trying to protect what they have.

Every business needs to make a reasonable profit. If a book seller must sell his books at pennies over what he paid for them he is not making a reasonable profit and will close up at some point. If a music and video store cannot sell products for more than they paid for them almost every time they are going to go away and fast. If a car dealer cannot sell cars for a reasonable profit and pay the salesman a reasonable commission, the dealership will close down. These are facts of life and business life in particular.

If the above paragraph proves one thing it says when those businesses close down the jobs they provided go away with them. Chances are those jobs lost because of the Internet are not coming back any time soon and probably not at all.

What this leaves America with is a host of new entrepreneurial jobs. Create your own; make it up as you go, no paycheck jobs dependent on the Internet to create a cash flow. No benefits, no paycheck, no meeting the public one-on-one and no real future. Yes you see the ads in your email box every day;

"How I made $4,778 a month from my home computer and never left my house" or "Make money from the leisure of your own home, I did and I'm now retired making $5,000 a month in income."

Eventually you will spend hundreds of dollars on information to get your "new business" up and running and you won't make $5,000 a month. Chances are within three months you will give up realizing the only people making money at this are those who solicited you on the Internet about these careers and got *your* money. Internet Scams are so prevalent the justice department can't keep up with them.

Changing the Way to the Internet

Fixing the problem of no barriers to entry is not going to be easy. In fact, many will tell you it doesn't need fixing, or, the market place will determine the fix. The truth of the matter is it does need fixing and while the market place will take care of some of the problems, in the end it is probably best suited for government to make things happen in terms of regulations. The industry itself must also take action.

"The population growing up with the Internet are really the ones who are going to have to change and regulate the Internet," says attorney Erik Syverson. "Rules? Most of my clients are small businesses anywhere from $1 million to $30 million in revenue and they need to come together and lobby congress for laws. You must put pressure on your legislatures to provide you some protection, the Chamber of Commerce, Small Business Associations; there is also a real knowledge gap."

Syverson adds things are changing and have changed so rapidly action must be taken sooner rather than later.

"I'm 34 and was basically in college around the time the Internet was born. People my age understand but we are still in a situation where most people who are businessmen don't even know the issues they are going to be afraid of. The Internet has come a long way in only 15 years and it has revolutionized the way we do business. Facebook made a billion dollars but Google made many billions. Myspace used to be the biggest thing and now it's dead, worthless and I still don't know how Twitter will make money."

Since the Internet is a global phenomena one might think the place to address the situation is really the United Nations. Syverson takes a different approach.

"It is interesting before you can say go to the United Nations and the world order you probably have to start with your own home and bring order to your home in America," he points out. "Before getting others to police it we must start here at home first. By and large there is no internet regulation."

Among the key issues of course is net neutrality and the issue of allowing people access and what an internet provider can charge and what they can charge for downloading. Everything from censorship to the commercial issues are paramount depending on who is doing the talking and from what point of view. Many people are not even aware when it comes to downloading movies and shows to their home computer from their internet provider that there is a limit to how much they can download. For instance, Time Warner may allow you to download "X" amount of megabytes per month per household while AT&T might allow you to download "Y" amount. After that they either charge you more or shut you off.

Dr. Pamela Falk teaches United Nations studies at Hunter College in New York and is the Resident UN correspondent and Foreign Affairs analyst for CBS Network Radio & TV at the United Nations. A distinguished lecturer and professor of international economics, she also writes a well-read blog. Dr. Falk says the United Nations may not be the place to solve the ever growing problems of the Internet, but the UN is beginning to formulate a framework for an international agreement on copyrights and trademarks. International conventions, like the Bene Convention for the Protection of Literary and Artistic Works, are out of date and were never meant to deal with the Internet."

At some point there will be controls placed on the Web although it might take years to accomplish.

"The regulation of the Internet is difficult because it involves international communications and satellites," Dr. Falk points out. "It is inevitable and necessary that there be regulations on the Internet. However, they have been slow in developing because the Internet is so fundamentally tied to free speech. It's been a labyrinth for regulators to get the good out of regulation."

She points out some companies in the United States have tried placing restrictions on the use of megabytes, after being free for many years. That was also seen, this time, by users, as restricting the Internet to people with more money and the concept of Internet use was to be affordable.

Everyone is hooked, the price goes up and now the poorer people on the planet won't be able to use it. This defeats the purpose of the internet. You had a great debate of cost of megabytes and information transfer but eventually more people saw they wanted to keep the universal nature of the Internet rather than restrict it to the rich.

As former President Bill Clinton pointed out, the internet has cost the world any number of jobs and some of those jobs won't come back. Falk says this is one of the issues of concern to the United Nations.

There are three basic classifications of nations with respect to the Internet. The first are the very poor nations with very little infrastructure. The Internet isn't much of a factor in these countries because many of them are struggling to get electricity let alone internet servers to use on laptops. The second group is the developing nations and, of course, the industrialized nations at the top of the food chain. The latter two are where the Internet has had the biggest impact when it comes to job losses.

Falk says that for the last two decades the U.N. and the World Bank have been pumping money into programs for the developing nations. The programs have been designed to allow 'mom and pop' entrepreneurs to start companies and employ lower wage workers. The amount of pay to the working class isn't a huge factor at first because these are people living in poor countries who now have jobs and a couple dollars in their pocket. There was also a growing middle management class handling everything from clerical to shipping to billing. And of course there were the owner/executives.

The development of the Internet has had the effect of damaging the middle income management group by replacing it with on-line services.

"Those companies can now order everything on-line and they begin to develop their clientele on line and except for physically putting together the dresses or whatever they are making they don't need any other employees," Falk points out. "The jobs for clerical for example have been diminished or eliminated and those jobs are not coming back."

The money by the way is not trickling down to the lower level employees in a vast number of cases. So the owners are making more, productivity is up and an entire class of workers is now out of work. It also means they are less likely to be involved in their community, politics, government service and charity work.

These eliminated or diminished positions were previously held by people who also rode the local social ladder, they spend money at restaurants, they buy at the local grocery store, they purchase more expensive clothing and they travel. In effect, people who re-circulated their money back into the community they live in.

"So essentially you are keeping a small moneyed class but eliminated the professional or management class, and therefore social mobility is decreased," said Falk. "They have eliminated jobs which will never come back."

The professor of international economics calls it the danger zone.

"In the danger zone would be countries in East Asia and Africa. Because of conflicts and sometimes because of poverty and population booms, the international community began 20 years ago to support micro-businesses that are just developing and are reliant on unskilled labor. These countries in the danger zone have almost entirely eliminated jobs that involve administrative work. So ordering the textiles or the food and setting up delivery systems and all of the pieces which go into transferring and sending money, the wiring of money, all of that has become very accessible on the Internet and has eliminated jobs. Except for the actual manual labor, many of the micro industry businesses have eliminated 50-percent of their employees over the last two decades. The money may be coming to those firms but it is not trickling down at all, that is the danger zone."

At the upper end of the spectrum are the developed or industrialized nations. Among these are the United States, Great Britain, Japan and many other European and Western countries where jobs have fled from and to the developing nations.

"The biggest effect on industrial countries has been through outsourcing," Falk said. "The ability to export an entire company and all its employees to where salaries are lower, has at a minimum been an advantage to the company, a loss of employment within the industrialized country. This was never possible before the Internet became an on-line sales bonanza."

Voice Over The Internet or VOIP has been a great help to companies wanting to cut costs and has made it much easier to outsource. Since VOIP is basically using the Internet for free as a phone service such as Skype, the cost of long distance phone calls from say Chile to New York has evaporated. There is no cost. You don't have to pay long distance phone bills anymore with VOIP. Phone companies are trying to adapt to that challenge and there is a big loss of jobs for those who cannot adapt. It also helps the company making the move to decide their move based on the bottom line not on jobs in the USA.

Some of the jobs you might not associate with being lost due to the internet might surprise you. Do you know a map maker for instance or a surveyor?

"Map makers have been hit very hard," according to Falk. "The only way to see what has changed is Google Earth or GPS which can so minutely see changes in borders, in sea coasts or erosion and borders. That is all indispensably done on the internet. The old time profession of people who got out their equipment to survey the land is really being taken over by the internet and those jobs are not coming back. These changes make new jobs in the Internet industry. Whether it is good or bad depends on where you are sitting, but it has killed certain industries."

Falk says to discredit the good the Internet has done would be foolish despite the drawbacks.

"No one who wants to promote jobs or growth in the international economy overall can responsibly say that the internet has not benefitted the world. It has. The only problem is the U.N. and individual countries have to deal with the massive dislocation of jobs as a result of the development of the Internet. With all the advances in society and inventions there is a downside and retraining and education are essential. The upside to the Internet is incredible. It has allowed the lower classes to communicate with their families in different countries without running up a phone bill; families have been reunited over long distances, a father and daughter perhaps, when someone gets ill. In the political spectrum the Internet revolution has revolutionized revolution."

The use of the Internet for political change has been an incredible development.. It was a shocking development for Dr. Falk who has covered international breaking news for decades.

"In 1979 I said that Fed Ex and DHL had revolutionized revolutions because the rebels in El Salvador and Nicaragua who were fighting despots got their messages out. The cell phone industry has grown that. The internet exploded it. More recently the Internet was a large force in the Arab Spring."

In Egypt certainly the opposition credits Face Book for helping overthrow Hosni Mubarak after 40 years in power. Clearly there are great benefits in terms of speech and democratic progress and even some aspects of the economy -- but the international community has yet to successfully deal with finding the balance. It's not for lack of desire. Dr. Falk says the United Nations has placed it at the forefront of its agenda, the issue of retraining poor nations.

"There are proposals floating around for a convention on Internet and Information Technology, it's the big topic," Falk said from her office at the U.N. "The first round divided the topic: First came the restriction on the freedom of speech when countries shut the Internet down; second, was the impact on jobs and productivity, particularly in developing countries. It is difficult because it is such a new phenomena."

Again she insists the world looks at the Internet as a good and powerful tool.

"There is a general perception that the Internet has been this wonderful development in terms of transformational changes in the world. The Arab Spring relied on it, getting information out on the crackdowns on the opposition. Information has improved and to some extent international fighting of crime has improved. The International Criminal Courts Prosecutor told me he can now get evidence more easily on genocide and this Is due to the Internet."

The dark side however goes even darker when it comes to crimes against humanity.

"The two biggest threats to the international community in the Internet age are hacking and cyber attacks on a political front and pirating on the economic front. That is where you do see some Conventions that are in the early stages. The US has several divisions of Homeland Security focused on trying to avoid cyber attacks. The FBI was hacked, the Immigration Service was hacked and the CIA was hacked. So the US is vulnerable."

If you remember the word "Wiki Leaks" you understand why hacking and cyber attacks are some of the biggest criminal trends to confront the world. The UN is trying to deal with those through conventions and getting everyone to sign on to share information on criminals who attack a company or a country. Information sharing is key. The CIA and FBI, Interpol and MI-6 are probably the best at trying to share information when criminals are in cyberspace at an unknown physical location. Pooling information is a key subject of many UN efforts from conventions to resolutions to try and combine information sources. It is on a multilateral basis with five or six countries but the UN benefits from the international effort.

"In the years from 2000-2006, the use of the Internet spiked and criminal terror organizations such as Al Qaeda began to use the Internet," Falk said. "They were able to use the Internet to send information on their movements and then complete their criminal activity. In the case of Al Qaeda they used it to recruit. But law enforcement world wide figured it out and quickly how to track IP addresses and used it to their advantage."

With the attacks of 9-11, the Internet changed and tracking of messages between networks became essential. In terms of criminal networks both of terror and simple crime networks (such as drug and human trafficking) law enforcement used the Internet to find missing persons and track crime.

This is why when Osama bin Laden was living in Pakistan he didn't use the Internet or a cell phone and it was one of his foot messengers who was making a cell phone call which did him in. So the ability of the criminal activity to prosper on the Internet has greatly decreased but it is still uncontrollable.

Who hasn't received a message from a Nigerian businessman asking your help in freeing up his tens of millions of dollars and who is willing to give you a decent cut of that money if you allow him to use your bank to transfer the money? Despite the fact it is a well known scam the FBI warns it remains one of the bigger successful scams on the Internet. How many times a day do you have to clean out your SPAM box when trying to read your email? How many of those scams still make it past the filters to your INBOX?

"And many countries still try to keep the Internet at a minimum or restricted to authorized persons to control their people," added Falk. "Most people don't realize Cuba for example allows almost no access to the Internet except for those who are authorized; China places restrictions on a piecemeal basis and Iran, during one of the biggest protests turned it off completely."

There are other nations as well which at least restrict if not completely control the Internet.

"This is where the U.N. in many ways is trying to shed light on those restrictions. There are Security Council Resolutions around which condemn the shutting down of information flows. In the General Assembly there is a move to begin work on a Convention prohibiting restricting access to the Internet."

The United Nations however remains concerned about the global economic impact and will eventually find a way to regulate the Web to benefit the world economy.

"Every step along the way raises new questions, for example the release of classified information such as Wiki Leaks, and at each stage the national and international debate will take some discussion," Falk the historian points out. "Individuals have to determine what is involved in the greater social contracts as some earlier philosophers called it, in the use of cyberspace."

The historian pointed out how long it's taken what should have been a natural decision.

"It took 40 years to have a Convention to regulate the peaceful use of outer space and there was finally a convention at the U.N. Can anyone really regulate outer space beyond a countries own borders? The first thought is 'that is Big Brother.' No one can regulate the stratosphere but when people realized they don't want nuclear weapons and nuclear waste up there, and they realized countries were capable of putting their nuclear stockpiles in outer space the threat was such there was an International Convention. That is precisely what is happening with the Internet. The United Nations is grappling with putting restrictions while protecting the universality of it."

The bottom line is it still comes back to jobs.

"In the industrialized countries and most importantly in the middle countries there are different levels of impact. The poor are the least affected, the middle countries the developing industrialized countries are at a crisis point and the industrialized nations have been impacted and faced an international downturn because of the ripple effect on the rest of the world."

Whether it is the airwaves where radio and television signals travel, or the skies above us where giant jumbo jets pass overhead, there is a cost to doing business. Even if it is for safety (to protect those on the ground below, companies or private citizens from criminals) regulations have to be in place somewhere and somehow. Without them some would say only chaos and anarchy progress.

"The world has been trying to grapple with the contradictory need to protect freedom of speech and the flow of information on one hand and on the other hand the dramatic downturn of productivity and jobs the Internet has created," said Dr. Falk. "In developing countries the slowdown of work and the slowdown of job creation has been much more dramatic than industrial countries. It's because so much of the work done on the Internet is impacting the small business and the micro economy has been impacted the most."

Why It Will Never Be the Same Again

The simple truth to the matter is the world has caught up with the United States and isn't going to go backward again. Why should it?

In the late 1980's the United States was still the only major country living on the credit cycle, betting on the come so to speak. While the rest of the nations in the world were saving our own economists were telling us we were not. They said we needed to save and our rate of savings was well below our European counterparts.

We were a creditor nation as we pretty much always have been. We need something but don't have the money so we put it on a charge card. However, that "charge" card soon became a "credit card." A Charge Card was exactly as its name implied. We charged something and paid it off in full when the bill came. A Credit Card differed by reason of the fact you paid for something with the card because you didn't have the cash and then you paid it off in installments. The bank which owned the card charged you a small interest fee so you could borrow the money and pay it over time.

With a Charge Card you bought something for $100 and a month later you paid the issuing card company $100 and the item was yours. With the Credit Card you bought something for $100 and in a month you paid $10 while the bank which issued the card charged you $2 on the remaining $90 you owed. At this point you were paying $102 for the item you thought you bought for $100.

Several months later you still had not paid off the balance of $90 and the Card Company continued to tack on interest. Maybe a year or 15 months later you finally paid off the $100 item by paying $165 for it. The bank made money, the seller made money and you lost money. In all likelihood you put other things on that credit card as well and now you were carrying a balance of $500 and the interest was adding up.

In later years you got a second card to "transfer a balance" from the first card to the second which offered you "Free" interest for six months. You got a breather if you paid it off. Chances are you did not. You reasoned you saved six months worth of interest charges.

The United States was doing the same thing and Americans were caught up in it. The other nations in the world were not.

On my trips to Europe, including several to Italy in the period 1988-1993 I learned it was very difficult to use a credit card. Every travel book pointed out where to find the American Express Office in Rome. This was where you could easily exchange your checks and cash for local money, Lire. You bought travelers checks before you left the United States and you usually purchased some foreign currency. In this case it was Lire. I would typically take $500 in American Express Travelers Checks, $500 in Lire, $300 in American dollars and a credit card just in case. I never used the credit card on those early trips because no one would take it. It was all cash.

If you paid for your hotel they would take a check before they would take a credit card. They not only did not trust them, they rarely used them personally and therefore neither could the traveler. Europe was strong financially although it was not without its own problems. The biggest of which were the multiple currencies.

For centuries and since the fall of the Roman Empire, Europe cried out, nay begged for a common currency. If you traveled from Italy to France you had to exchange your Lire for Francs. If you traveled from France to Germany you had to change your Francs for Deutschemarks. If you looked in the seller's cash register near the border you would see a very large tray with various bills in various denominations from various countries. It truly was an insane way of doing things.

Enter the European Union and the Euro pushed by none other than the banks. Why would the banks be pushing for consolidation of the money system? It would end the bookkeeping nightmare thus saving costs. It would make it easier to move money around therefore cutting costs. It would make it easier to lend money, therefore making the banks money.

The Internet would eventually make it so simple to transfer money from one country to the other in small denominations (PayPal etc.) it was a wonder why it took so long for Rome to emerge again. Julius Caesar never thought it would be this easy while trying to conquer Gaul.

There were other reasons too some would conjecture. Credit. If people in Europe could so easily exchange money and put some trust in the banks to handle this new Euro then ushering in credit cards would be a no brainer. By 1994 the way to get cash in Europe was a little machine on nearly every corner called the Bank-A-Matic. In reality the ATM (Automatic Teller Machine) had arrived and taken Europe by storm.

Make no mistake about it this was a "debit" card system but in a light years time was turned into the "Credit Card." Before long Europeans were just like the rest of us in the good old USA, creditors tied to the credit card. Today nearly every person in Europe has a credit card and just like Americans is fighting their way out of debt.

The housing market would never have crashed in Europe if it wasn't for cheap credit. We expect it in America because we know of nothing else. In Europe and now the rest of the world, Credit has over taken Cash as king. It isn't going back because the banks won't let it.

All this is coming more to light as you look at the recent 2011 settlement regarding American Express. A class action suit sent about $100 to travelers who were overcharged in currency transactions involving American Express cards. When it was Europe 1988 very few people even thought of taking American Express, Visa or MasterCard. The only card considered was Diners Club and it was really only for high end places and rarely if ever used by the average traveler.

While American Express denied any wrongdoing it was accused of colluding with Visa and MasterCard to set fees for converting purchases made in foreign currencies. In a separate case several other banking institutions agreed to pay more than $275 million to consumers for allegedly hiding fees. The banks involved were Bank of America, MBNA, Chase, Citibank, HSBC/Household, Washington Mutual/Providian, Bank One/First USA, Diners Club, Visa and MasterCard. They all denied any wrongdoing. Consumers got about $25 each for that case.

Now that the world is on the same system as the United States it isn't going to turn back and as already proven the banks are not going to let go of a good thing; money made on the interest paid by the masses. They can't and they won't.

If the world had kept itself free of the American form of individual credit via the credit card the world economy would be much stronger and the great depression or recession as some like to call it which started with the market crash of October 2008, would likely never have happened.

For the great American economy to rebound and lead the world in the way it did before the 1990's the world would have to give up its credit demands. First of all it is not possible given the breadth of the credit mess in the world and more importantly the usage of credit by the individual, but there are those who say it should not go back. There are some economists who believe the current system is the only way for the world economy to operate and if that is true we are really in a sad state of affairs.

What it means is there must be a new concentration on a new world economic order and man does not have the stomach or the will for that issue and the banks won't allow it even if he did.

Epilogue: Where Do We Go From Here?

Let me point out first and foremost overall the Internet as we know it is a wonderful thing and it is not going away. It is a place where change constantly occurs and everyone must adapt in some way. Whether it is business, personal or social everyone must adapt to life on the Internet.

The most recent battle between the United States Congress and the SOPA and PIPA legislation only highlighted the battle which will continue over where the Internet should go from this point forward. Both bills, pushed by big business and especially those companies which see copyright infringement through piracy as stealing from them (as it is) versus those large companies and consumers who want the Internet to remain with fewer controls not more. The Senate was all set to vote on the bills when Google and Wikipedia encouraged web surfers to pound Congress with protests. Wikipedia took itself down for about a day in protest.

They got the attention of Congress and the bills were taken off the floor and there was talk of a compromise much to the chagrin of Hollywood. Hollywood and the music industries are the most damaged by piracy. It was just days earlier the authorities working in conjunction pulled down an Australian site which basically was allowing file sharing of pirated products. Megaupload.com made millions of dollars doing what they were doing.

There are those who say we have enough control over the Internet and these pieces of legislation smack of Big Brother-ism. Even the liberal comedian and talk show host Bill Mahr on his HBO show *"Real Time"* blasted those who steal. He also seemed to support those who speak on behalf of those bills to some degree. Mahr claimed to have lost millions of dollars when pirates copied and sold his feature film about religion. His comment was "just because you're sitting at your computer in your pajama bottoms doesn't mean you're not stealing," and when it came to those who do such things "we still want free sh-t – that's what they were saying."

Basically Internet users don't really care where they get what they get, who stole it and who made it and who should be paying for it. They just want it and they don't really want to pay for it. This, in the end analysis amounts to "theft."

In a few years everyone in the world will have some sort of on-line presence. Those who have resisted the Internet because they either feared it or fight change in everything they have done will be dead. The Internet generation, those born post 1992 who don't know life without the Internet, will rule the world and information flowing to all parts of it. This is a fact no one can deny.

It is perhaps for their sake, those of us who lived life before the Internet age; need to act to make sure an orderly world exists after we are long gone from this earth. The Internet has been described as the Wild West. Even the Wild West adapted and changed for the better. Lawless life was forced out and placed under the control of new rules and laws and new lifestyles.

The Internet must do the same. There must be a cost to doing business and whether that cost is via rules and regulations, fees, or licensing there will be a cost. What that cost is has yet to be determined. Freedom is a responsibility whether it is economic freedom or freedom of choice but it is a responsibility, and being responsible on the Internet and with the Internet must be a part of the World Wide Web experience. We must fully understand that Free is a wonderful thing to live. Free is not a wonderful thing in the business world.

####

www.ingramcontent.com/pod-product-compliance
Lightning Source LLC
Chambersburg PA
CBHW071417170526
45165CB00001B/302